First published 1976 by
Octopus Books Limited
59 Grosvenor Street, London W1

©1976 Octopus Books Limited

ISBN 0 7064 0550 1

Produced by Mandarin Publishers Limited
22a Westlands Road, Quarry Bay, Hong Kong

Printed in Hong Kong

ELV

PETER

VIS

JONES

ACKNOWLEDGEMENTS

The publishers would like to thank the following individuals and organizations for their kind permission to reproduce the photographs in this book:

Camera Press 42 below right, 74, 77 right; Globe Photos 88, (Don Dornan) 30; Laurens van Houten 64–5, 67 left, 67 right; John Kingaby 21 left, 13, 44–5, front jacket; Kobal Collection 3 left, 22 left, 38, 40, 56, 57, 58 below left, 58 centre, 61, 72 right; Photoreporters Inc. (Phil Roach) 80; Popperfoto 4 inset right, 14, 15, 22 right, 42 centre left, 43 above left, 48 below left, 43 right, 48–9, 58–9, 62 below left, centre left and centre right, 84–5, back flap; RCA 2 right, 5, 26–7, 28–9, 30–1, 69, 77 centre; Rex Features 1, 3 right, 8, 9, 16–17, 20, 24, 34–5, 47, 52, 54, 55, 62 above, 67 centre, 72 left, 73, 75, 77 left, 81, 85 inset, 86–7, back jacket, front flap, (Bob Patrick) 70; Syndication International 50–1; Transworld Feature Syndicate 63, 82–3; Universal Pictorial Press 58 above left, 78; Paul Wakefield endpapers.

The publishers would like to give especial thanks to many American sources for their material.

HUMBLE

ELVIS Presley was born on 8 January 1935, shortly after midday, in a tiny house in East Tupelo, one of the poorer parts of Mississippi. He was born in the front room, the bedroom, on an iron bedstead which stood, lumpy mattress and all, on bare floorboards.

It was a tough delivery. As Elvis Aaron let out his first lusty bellows, his mother, Gladys felt something was wrong. The doctor stood by as she gasped for air as though she was still in labour.

Even she hadn't realized that she was to have twins. She'd had no warning, but then medical diagnosis was not very sophisticated in East Tupelo.

An hour or so later a second baby was born, but he was dead. Within another couple of hours Jesse Garon was laid out in a tiny coffin, and the next day he was buried in what remains an unmarked grave in a hillside cemetery.

So Elvis Presley, destined to become the greatest single figure in the pop-rock world, remained an only child, and on him were lavished the love and affection that but for the tragedy would have been shared between two.

There is so much room for conjecture. Had Jesse Garon Presley lived, would he have had a stake in the Presley talent? Would they have operated as

BEGINNINGS

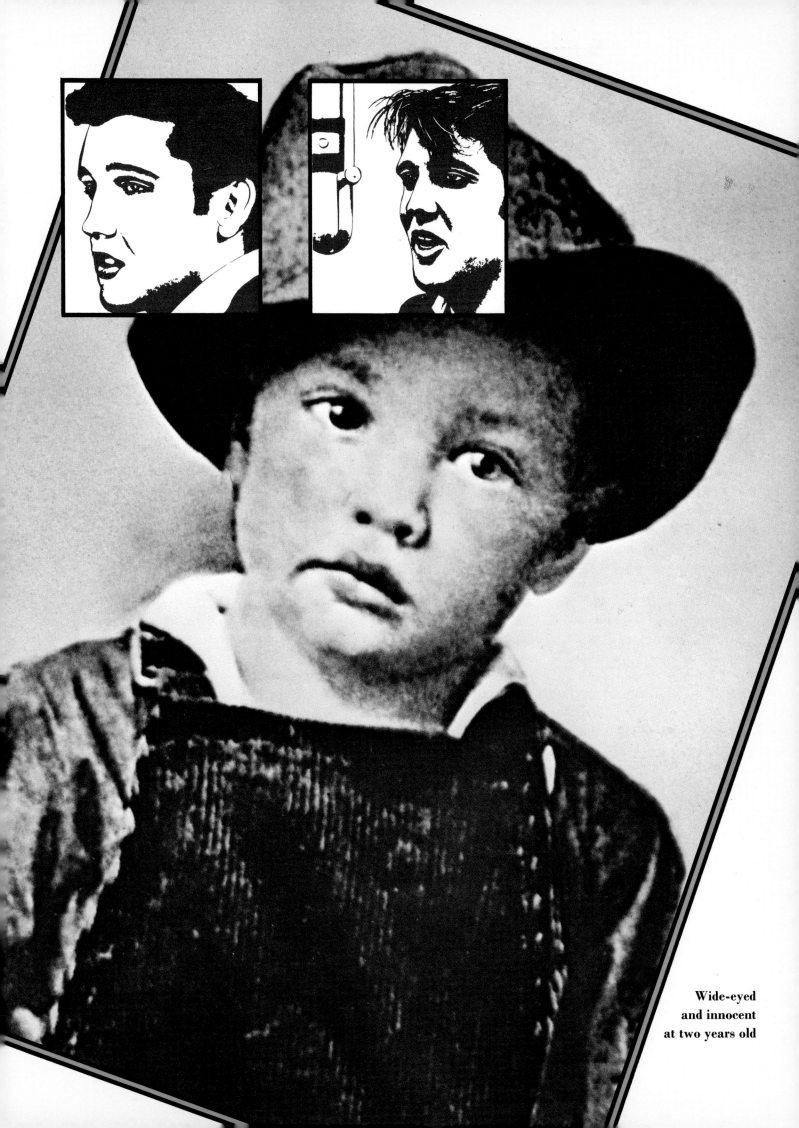

Wide-eyed and innocent at two years old

an identical-twin act, in a sense doubling the pleasure the Presley family was to give to the world?

One can only guess at what might have happened. The cold facts of the Presley career are that today he is one of the wealthiest entertainers in the world; his earnings are put at $40 million a year, from new records, consistent re-releases, movies, merchandising and personal appearances; and he can earn $250,000 for just two performances.

A group of international show-business experts were invited to list nominations for an all-time 'great' roster of stars who had contributed to the development and progress of pop music. Finally a list of five emerged.

Al Jolson, chronologically, came first for the way he'd injected showmanship into the popular ballad and also for his involvement with the first 'all-talking, all-singing' movies. His first acknowledged million seller was 'The Spaniard That Blighted My Life', recorded in 1913. His classic, 'Sonny Boy', came out in 1928. He died in 1950.

Next was Bing Crosby who, according to most reference books, is the most successful record seller of all. Certainly he took the 'starch' out of popular singing – he once said: 'If I sound relaxed, it's because I'm bone idle.' His biographer Charles Thompson suggested: 'Crosby is probably the most popular character in the world, outside of Walt Disney characters.'

Certainly Crosby was to receive a platinum disc in 1960 to commemorate 200 million sales of his 2,600 singles and 125 albums. Now he has doubled that total. But Crosby started recording in the early 1930s and, four decades on, was still going strong both in the recording studios and on the golf course.

Next on the list of all-time greats came Frank Sinatra. He was included because he again changed the face and the sound of pop music. He inspired the original bobbysox scene, with fans screaming for him, clawing at him and swooning at the mere sound of his voice. He was known as The Voice, was a one-time band singer (Harry James and Tommy Dorsey) who went solo via radio and moved successfully into Hollywood movies.

Fourth on the list was Presley, and it should be stressed that this is an in-order-of-appearance rating. The Beatles came fifth, the only group included but deservedly there for the Merseybeat explosion that was to change pop music so drastically in 1963.

The Beatles were to become, in a comparatively short time, the biggest-selling group in history, and John Lennon and Paul McCartney were the top songwriting team of the 1960s. But the Beatles were to disband, their 40,000-strong British fan club closing down in 1972 when it became obvious the four from Liverpool would never get together again.

Which left Elvis Presley the most notable survivor of modern pop history. A list of just some of his achievements proves the point:

'Heartbreak Hotel', backed with 'I Was The One', was Number One in the States for eight weeks in 1956.

By February 1961, Presley had sold $76 million worth of records. In 1956 he sold ten million

records and earned a million dollars from royalties. He had records at Number One in the States for 25 weeks through that year, and was top for 24 weeks the next year.

He'd been hailed in Britain and Europe following publicity referring to him as 'the American kid with the platinum-plated tonsils'. By 1970, he'd sold 160 million disc units.

And he'd won more Gold Discs (for sales of a million-plus) than anybody else.

In every way, the Presley influence was felt in pop music, and for countless big pop performers of today, Elvis Presley has been the inspiration. John Lennon said right at the height of Beatlemania: 'My one crushing ambition in life was to be as big as Elvis Presley.' He has never said whether he thought he has made it.

By the time Elvis got to his 40th birthday in 1975, the one-time theatre usher and truck driver had been a recording artist for twenty years and was still a chart 'regular' throughout the world. His popularity is reflected in the membership figures of his fan clubs in every country where pop music is played.

And yet in many ways he'd done it all wrong. Despite his non-stop success, Presley has taken risks, both in his career and in his private life. Pop music is, with good reason, regarded as one of the most chancy areas of entertainment. It was fine for the old stalwarts like Jolson, Sinatra and Crosby. They hit an across-the-board audience, but mostly their balladeering and love-song crooning were aimed at audiences made up of the middle-aged and the old.

Presley crashed right into a teenage market – in fact he virtually created that market. And as many other pop-rockers experienced after Presley, that market was to prove itself very fickle. Some singers were dropped for no better reason than that they'd got married, so becoming unavailable to the fans. Some hit a downward slide simply because the record buyers got fed up with them.

But despite breaking the rules, Presley somehow grew with the development of pop. At first he was the rough-and-ready leader of a new excitement, continually criticized by the establishment who deplored the fan hysteria he stirred up and reacted even more violently to the way he suggested blatant sexuality in the hip-swivelling movements he moulded to the lyrics.

Now he is a kind of elder statesman pop-style, and his audiences have changed simply because most of them have grown up with him. Certainly they've never abandoned him, left him for dead. Every so often it looks as if Presley has finally cracked up, and could even retire gracefully. Then he hits back with a stunning stage or television show, or a hit record, and it is as if he'd never been away.

Yet, technically speaking, he did it all wrong. The kid from Mississippi was influenced by black men's music, by the blues. He took that music, injected a little Gospel touch here and there, and he sang it. Not just as a white man's adaptation, but as a musical style which transcended all ethnic considerations. He even sounded like a black man. His early records on the Sun label in Memphis had a rockabilly roughness to them which to an extent 'fooled' the folk who ran the local radio stations and hired out the jukeboxes.

For in those days, there was black music and white music, and the two were not supposed to meet. There were barriers. White artists didn't get on black-music radio stations. White artists didn't even visit black-music clubs.

Presley, however, was to prove himself a true original in that he became acceptable – instantly – in all markets. Black and white . . . and then in country and western, and rhythm and blues, and ordinary plain down-to-earth pop.

He was to lose much of that early rough-and-raw vocal style once he became a polished superstar, but he did not lose those early fans. They still buy his records today, while searching for his old originals (and paying up to £100 each for them).

As for his explosively athletic performance style . . . well, there's room later to describe just how much that upset police authorities, teachers and the church. Elvis Presley clearly possessed the most controversial hip-wiggle in history.

But in fact he learned how to wiggle in a most unlikely place – in church. A church goer as a kid, Elvis used to clamber down off his mother's knee and

Elvis and Priscilla on their wedding day, 1 May 1967 and (right) in Las Vegas two years later

run down the aisle towards the church platform. And if he didn't know the words it didn't matter, because he still got caught up in the rhythm. He says now:

We'd often be in these religious singings, with folk all joining in and expressing themselves through their hymns. But there would be these singers, perfectly fine singers in their own style, but they just couldn't get the congregations going.

It was all kinda stiff and starchy. And then you'd get the preachers, travelling preachers a lot of them, and they'd cut up all over the place, jumpin' on the piano, movin' every which way. The audience liked them and responded to the sheer energy of it all.

So the movements which churchmen were to put down as 'morally depraved' and 'obscene' actually originated from the church itself. But, of course, church services in the Tupelo evangelistic First Assembly of God Church were more lively than in Beverly Hills, California, or Manhattan, New York.

But Presley still hadn't finished with his 'wrong-doing'. He got himself a manager, one Colonel Tom Parker, who was destined to match his pride-and-joy artist by becoming the most controversial manager in the business.

When Elvis Presley really hit the big time, he was not allowed to follow the usual well-trodden pop trail – that is, world tours, cashing in fast because the career might be over in double-quick time. Presley toured a little in the States, but the rest of the world has never got to see him.

The original show-business maxim was: 'Always leave an audience wanting more.' Colonel Parker rewrote it as: 'Don't show yourself to the audience at all and they'll want more for a darned sight longer.'

So Presley just made records and he made films. And still his popularity didn't waver at all. Twenty years on there are fans around the world who kid themselves that one day he'll set out to visit them.

That decision, arguable on a number of different grounds, could easily have put paid to Presley's popularity. And so could the way he accepted his two-year stint as a guest of the United States Army. From 1958 to 1960 he wore uniform, and yet not for a moment lost his leadership of the pop world.

But Presley, for millions a kind of rebel figure, refused to rebel against Army discipline. He had his hair cut, polished his boots until they shone like jewels, and 'got some in' as an exemplary recruit. Even

his drill instructor, a gnarled master sergeant named Henry Coley, couldn't fault the parade-ground-stamping Presley.

Yet a lot of the Presley fans felt the hero should have slammed back at authority and the establishment. There were his songs, his records, sometimes his movies, stirring up all kinds of teenage energy and there was the leader, saluting all and sundry, and even doing well enough to become a sergeant himself, commanding a three-man reconnaissance team for the Third Armored Division's 32nd Scout Platoon.

Yet when he returned to the States, to pick up the threads of his career again, still a giant figure in pop music, still the guv'nor, he found he'd gained the respect of the establishment, but lost nothing of his popularity among the fans.

Now the 1960s were a time when pop heroes had to be 'available' as far as the fans were concerned. Girls had to believe there was just a chance, just a slender hope, that they might get to meet, make and marry the star. It surely did happen, even outside the Hollywood musical scene. But once the star had got married, had posed for starry-eyed pictures of wedded bliss, then he became 'unavailable' and the fans moved on to somebody else. That was the theory anyway.

**On stage in Kansas City, 1956 with the old team:
Bill Black on bass, Scotty Moore on guitar and
J. D. Fontana on drums**

Once again Elvis Presley defied the accepted rules of pop stardom. He married Priscilla Ann Beaulieu, a stunningly attractive brunette of 21, a girl who'd grown up in Memphis, Tennessee, but had really got to know Elvis in Germany during his Army service. She'd met the man who then was the most famous soldier in the whole army at a party. They got married on 1 May 1967. Journalists, bemused by this apparent defiance of pop-star custom, asked Elvis why he'd decided to turn his back on bachelordom.

He replied: 'Bachelordom'.

They persisted, pointing out that the marriage could harm his career future. Elvis replied: 'I'm getting married because I figured it was about time.'

True, there were times when Elvis didn't sell as many records as usual. But always he fought back. Right across the years, new superstars emerged, many saying they wanted to emulate the Presley success story . . . and that they'd been much influenced by him. Bob Dylan was one. Marc Bolan another. And when Bruce Springsteen emerged in 1975 as a big new star, he left interviewers in no doubt about his views.

He said: 'Presley was the guy who turned me on. Anyone who says they can hear Presley or see him and not be turned on by him just has to be deficient up top. I defy anybody, with any music in him not to be affected by Elvis Presley.'

And Alvin Stardust, with two stabs at fame (as Shane Fenton in the 1960s and again in his reincarnation in the 1970s), admits: 'What spurred me on to try for success in pop was Presley. I'd stand for hours in front of a mirror, holding a tennis racquet and pretending I was him. All his movements, the sneer, the pout – even his hairstyle.'

Yet all the way along the line, Elvis has broken rules, done things which in a lesser personality would have had him either run out of town or at least out of the business.

And he's done it on two things: strength of personality and that unique, deep-throated, sexy, insinuating voice and vocal style. Just so long as he's looked good and sung well, he's made fortune after fortune.

While Dylan, for example, gets a lot of his income from his songwriting, Elvis has invariably relied upon others to write his songs for him. While Elvis is around, there's always a chance for a young, unknown songwriter to get famous (and rich) by having Elvis record one of his songs.

Nor is Elvis much of an instrumentalist. True, in popularity polls over the years he's been placed high in the 'best guitarist' sections, but that's more through

fan loyalty than talent.

He survived divorce, a very costly arrangement when it finally happened. He even made a dramatic return to live shows after a gap of nine long years – and made the audience that evening feel he'd never been away.

And he said then: 'I'm really glad to be back in front of a live audience. I don't think I've ever been more excited than I was tonight.'

He earned a fee of £225,000 (yes, pounds not dollars) for that show. But it was the atmosphere of the evening, the drama of the return of the prodigal, that got through to him – not the size of the cheque.

And with that return from what Elvis called 'my personal wilderness' he was back into another string of non-stop hits.

That kind of resilience and style is what has made Elvis Presley the greatest single figure in pop music over the years. He's been derided and admired; hated and loved. But mostly there's been love.

The detailed story of how he has made it through so many different crazes in music – Beatles, Stones, Monkees, flower power, psychedelic, teenybop, progressive, light, heavy, good and bad – is fascinating. And the man himself is fascinating. It all started way down in Tupelo, Mississippi . . .

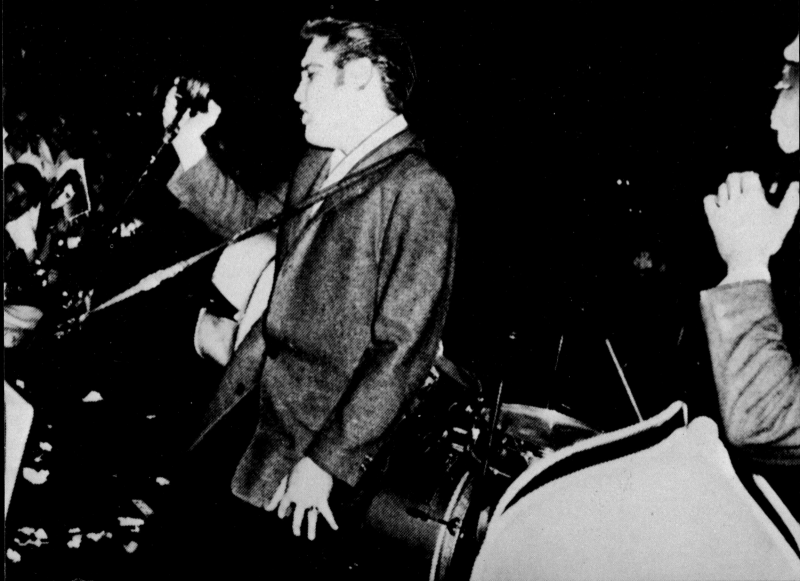

MOVING TO

BACK in 1935, East Tupelo was nobody's idea of heaven. It was an area of cottonfields and sugar plantations. Black folk and white worked on the plantations because there wasn't much else to do.

So the workforce hoed the corn patches and tidied up the pea beds and attended to the cottonfields. Prayers spiralled upwards every day that nothing would happen to spoil the crops.

Vernon Presley, Elvis's father, had learned a lot about the heartbreaking economics of farm life in East Tupelo. He'd done his share of the backbreaking work, too – toiling from sun-up to sun-down, barely scratching out a living.

He met Gladys Smith, four years older than himself, on a visit to the main centre of East Tupelo. Their feelings for each other were deep . . . and instant. They married and for a while lived with their in-laws, switching from the Presleys to the Smiths, making sure they never outstayed their welcome at either place.

But in the summer of 1934, Gladys Presley knew for sure she was pregnant. She also knew she had to give up her job as a sewing-machine operator in the local garment factory, even though this would stretch the family budget to the limit. Nothing was to get in the way of a safe birth for the child they both wanted so badly, and a working life of six days a week, twelve hours a day, tied by invisible tapes to a sewing machine was no way to go through a pregnancy.

The Presleys were luckier than most, because Vernon's boss was a kindly man who did what he

could, when he had the money, to help his workers. He helped the Presleys get the tiny house in which Elvis Aaron Presley was to be born, a healthy, chubby-cheeked baby, and his twin brother, Jesse Garon, was to be born dead.

It wasn't much of a home, but it was better than the shacks and shanties where most local workers lived. There was no running water – just a pump, a short run away. Built entirely of wood, poorly furnished, the house just about did its job of keeping the often fierce Mississippi elements at bay.

Elvis was brought up to show dignity and courtesy, despite the morale-sapping poverty of the neighbourhood. As an only child, there's no argument that he was spoiled. Family friends noted how Gladys Presley doted on her son, rarely letting him out of her sight. He was a chubby, blond-haired child with well-rounded and staring eyes. Not particularly handsome, but a pleasant little boy who treated other people with respect, always saying 'sir' and 'ma'am' and full of pleases and thank-yous.

All the pictures of Elvis taken in those years of early childhood show the upper lip curled into what appears to be a snarling sneer. It twisted downwards, whether the boy was being serious or smiling. It was to become one of the best-known trademarks in the history of pop music.

The Presleys, Vernon and Gladys, had both been religious folk from childhood. Near their home was the Church of the First Assembly of God where they worshipped every Sunday. It was there, in the

MEMPHIS

Dallas, October 1956: as wild as ever . . .

sometimes frantic services featuring visiting evangelists, that Elvis Presley heard his first music.

This was real firebrand religion. It was based on the premise that you have to be good or go straight to hell, there to burn forever in torment. It was Bible-thumping, breast-beating religion. And it held Elvis's attention from the very start.

As they sat in the cramped one-floor church, the Presleys looked like any other local family, decked out in Sunday best: the father tall, straightbacked, clear-eyed, the mother strikingly beautiful, with expressive eyes. And Elvis, usually quiet and reserved, . but sometimes fairly hopping around with excitement.

His mother, interviewed years later about her son the superstar, recalled:

I'd have to keep my eyes on him the whole time through one of those services, otherwise he'd hop off my lap before I could stop him and he'd be off down the aisle.

He'd gaze up at the choir and do his best to join in the singing. He'd wave his arms with excitement. Of course he was too young to know any of the words, but there's no denying that that

was when music first got into his soul.

By the time Elvis was six, things were no easier for the Presley family in terms of earning money. Elvis was still very much the apple of his mother's eye, and at school, he was an alert, willing, enthusiastic student. He'd march across to the wooden school-house, the East Tupelo Consolidated School, invariably hand-in-hand with his mother.

There were maybe 800 students in the school, and Elvis was constantly reminded how important it was for him to get a good education, as a kind of passport from the poverty of East Tupelo – and he was warned not to waste his time in class.

When classes were over for the day, he'd march back home, again with his mother, and he'd relate what had happened. True to her religious beliefs, Mrs Presley taught him that it was better to talk his way out of trouble than to try to punch his way out. 'Fighting is for the ignorant,' she said.

At school, Elvis managed to avoid the usual scuffles and playground fights. The fact was that he looked rather too angelic to get involved in the usual punch-ups. It seemed to his proud parents that Elvis was getting prettier and prettier with each passing year.

But at school he started using his voice to entertain others.

Each day started with a short religious service for the kids. Each day the teachers would ask if anybody wanted to say a special prayer for the others. Elvis preferred to sing. He knew several hymns, but one song – 'Old Shep' – was his particular favourite. It is a sugary, sentimental pop-type song, and not all that suited to a religious service, but when Elvis sang it he held his audiences spellbound.

To this day he includes the song in his act. It's his own special reminder of his days at school.

He so impressed the principal teachers that Elvis found himself entered in the talent section of the Mississippi and Alabama Fair and Dairy Show. It was very much an agricultural sort of get-together, but during the 1940s the talent contest became a sort of bonus.

It was 1945, and Elvis was ten, when he first took part – representing his home town. He sang 'Old Shep', unaccompanied, and standing on a chair. The Red Foley song earned him huge applause, and he loved every moment of it.

Elvis has said since, 'If I had to pinpoint a moment in time when I knew I had to make a life in show business it was then. Besides, the money came in mighty useful.'

In fact he got only second prize. Five dollars,

plus tickets letting him go free on most of the amusement rides.

In between school and church, Elvis listened to the local radio stations. There was plenty to hear. White music was intended just for the white man – it was melodic, country-styled, high on love-lost, love-won content. And black music was for the black man, with its heavier beat, and its foot-tapping rhythms.

Elvis soaked it all up. Later he was to prove a real musical trail-blazer by getting the two musical sources together, blending them into one multi-million dollar industry. He was the white man singing the black man's music. In doing so, he was proving more adroit at integration than many governments and politicians had been.

Listening to so much music made Elvis want to play for himself. Banging out rhythms on a table-top wasn't much to satisfy his artistic inclinations, so one Christmas he had to make a very important decision: he could either have a bicycle as a present – or a guitar.

He chose the guitar, which pleased his parents because the bicycle was four times as expensive. He taught himself to play a few chords while listening to the radio, and two of his uncles, one on his mother's side and the other on his father's showed him a little more.

Today Elvis can remember with pleasure the artists who did a lot to shape his own style. There were white country artists like Jimmy Rodgers and Roy Acuff, along with Ernest Tubb, one of the most revered figures in the field.

Across the 'barrier', on the black side, he found himself identifying with blues men like Big Bill Broonzy, Otis Spann, John Lee Hooker, and, in particular, a Mississippi musician named Arthur Big Boy Crudup.

Country music, rhythm and blues, and moments of pure gospel in church – Elvis may have been short on a lot of material things as a kid but he was in precisely the right place to absorb many different musical influences.

So Elvis toted his guitar round the neighbourhood, playing it wherever he could. He'd strum it so enthusiastically that the strings were always breaking and, being short of pocket money, he'd often have to practise with three or four strings instead of the usual six.

More influences came when the family moved for a short while to a little shack nearer the black ghetto of the area. But the most important move was to be when Vernon Presley finally hit his own ambition target . . . and hoisted the family to Memphis, Tennessee.

. . . and still rocking: Los Angeles the same year

It was no triumphant departure. As Elvis recalls:

We hadn't more than a couple of bucks between us. Just a beat-up old Plymouth, with a full gas tank, and all our belongings strapped to the roof. We didn't have no big hopes of finding those Memphis streets paved with gold. All we knew, and I remember it well, was that wherever we went it sure had to be better than life in Tupelo.

What first frightened the Presleys in Memphis, biggest city in the whole state of Tennessee was the sheer size of the place. The buildings, streets, and shopping centres made it seem as if they'd just come from some Lilliputian township.

They started their bright new life in a one-room apartment. Just to get to the bathroom meant a long trek up stairs and along corridors.

Elvis Presley, in his teens, was a shy person who hated being put in a position where he had to meet strangers. Being in Memphis, Tennessee, meant he was completely surrounded by strangers. When he had to report to the L. C. Humes High School in Memphis, he admits his knees were knocking – 'and I felt like

15

the hair on my head was standing straight up through sheer fright.'

Elvis had this deep-down fear that big-city kids would laugh at him, because of his accent and his clothes. Most of the other kids did have more money to spend, and the Presleys were still just eking out an existence – with Vernon on shift-work in a tool company and Gladys sometimes earning a few extra dollars by waiting on table in a local diner.

For Elvis, school life started with what he regarded as a dreadful rejection. They wouldn't even let him sing, one voice among many, in the school choir. They said he just didn't have the kind of voice that would fit into a choir, and they said it in a way that left no doubt that that was criticism and not a compliment. Having long believed he could sing quite well, no matter what else he couldn't do, Elvis inevitably took an anti-establishment stand against the 'they' involved.

He was, at sixteen, a quiet-spoken and extremely polite boy, who seemed the kind of lad who didn't want to be any trouble to anyone. In the end he did start making friends, dating a few girls and, almost without realizing it, absorbing the ways of the big city.

Whenever he had some money saved up, he'd buy himself some flash Memphis-style clothes. His long hair was out of style in those days, but he insisted on keeping it flowing, there in the middle of acres of stubbly crew-cuts. When he dressed up to go on a date, there was a touch of arrogance about him which somehow was at variance with the politeness and charm he usually displayed.

And still he toted that guitar around, playing for his friends, or doing a star turn at picnics and barbecues. His obvious ability to put over a song, and that distinctive blend of musical styles, made him a popular kid, even if he often gave the impression he was a loner.

He'd never take any of his friends back home. For the Presley apartment, on Poplar Avenue, was in

no kind of shape to be a base for entertaining. Often the local sanitary and health people would call round, to make checks on the conditions. In the end, the local authorities decided to move the Presleys into a federal-financed apartment in a block called Lauderdale Courts. For the family this was the height of luxury – two bedrooms, nicely decorated, and all for around thirty dollars a month.

But again it was very much a mixed area. The whites occupied one part just opposite a ghetto where the blacks lived in the direst conditions. The one source of entertainment in that ghetto was music. Self-made music. Music tapped out on old boxes, on home-made string basses. Hip-writhing music that provided at least a temporary release from lives of abject poverty.

The keen-eared Elvis Presley soaked up all that music, too. And in the evenings he'd rehearse what he'd heard. His style was becoming more and more distinctive. His voice grew deeper and more mellow. And when he sang, he found himself swinging his whole body to the music.

At moments like that, it was as if he had been taken over totally by the music. He recalls: 'Right from those early days, my movements have been just natural. I just couldn't help myself. Even when I was just listening to the radio I couldn't keep myself still.'

Now it's 1951, a year into a decade that was to change the whole image of popular music. To appreciate just how great that change was, it is important to understand what pop was all about in the pre-Presley days.

The kind of records which earned Gold Discs – that is, for selling a million copies – in 1951, when Elvis was a city-dwelling sixteen-year-old – were by such singers as Rosemary Clooney, Doris Day, Eddie Fisher and Fred Astaire.

There were orchestral novelties, like 'The Syncopated Clock', by Leroy Anderson and his Pops concert orchestra. Nat King Cole was to strike gold with 'Too Young'. Patti Page was just about the biggest of the girl singers. Johnnie Ray was adding a touch of gimmickry – he was half deaf, half Red Indian and he produced real tears when singing his way into the charts with songs like 'Little White Cloud That Cried'.

Pop had its heroes who were screamed at by the fans. Bobbysoxers had swooned in the presence of Frank Sinatra back in the 1940s; fan reaction became that much more violent with the arrival of Johnnie Ray.

Country and western music, one of the big influences on Elvis Presley, was particularly popular. One 1951 million seller was Red Foley's 'Peace In The Valley', an inspirational gospel song. A little lad named Jimmy Boyd had a million seller with 'I Saw Mommy Kissing Santa Claus'. Vera Lynn, now Dame Vera Lynn, was proving her power of survival. She'd been dubbed the 'sweetheart of the forces' in the UK during World War II, with her morale-boosting songs like 'We'll Meet Again', and 'Bluebirds Over The White Cliffs of Dover', and in 1951 she struck gold in an unprecedented manner.

Vera Lynn cut a version of 'Auf Wiedersehen Sweetheart', with an orchestra directed by Roland Shaw and with a chorus of soldiers, sailors and airmen of the British Armed Services. It not only topped the charts in Britain but in the United States, too – the first-ever record to top the charts both sides of the Atlantic.

And that is what pop in the early 1950s was all about. Schmaltzy sentimental songs, often sung by 'fugitives' from the Hollywood movie-musical sound-stages, and gimmicky little numbers, performed dead straight.

Just occasionally a record hit the airwaves of the world that gave hope of a bluesy, rocking future.

One which appealed greatly to Elvis was Lloyd Price's 'Lawdy Miss Clawdy', which struck gold. Price wrote this song, having formed his own nine-piece band on discharge from the US Forces. This was authentic rhythm and blues. Elvis also liked Ruth Brown's 'Five, Ten, Fifteen Hours' – she was a coloured girl who had roots deep in the Gospel-singing church services of the deep south.

And he was very much into the style of Fats Domino, just about the biggest seller in the rhythm and blues field, whose recording of 'The Fat Man' did a lot to establish the New Orleans sound. Other million sellers around at this time were 'Goin' Home', 'Going To The River', 'You Said You Loved Me', 'Please Don't Leave Me' and 'I Lived My Life'.

Fats Domino was getting played mostly on the black radio stations,' but with each year the exposure given his records was more general. Elvis Presley didn't know it then but he was to play a big part in gaining really wide recognition for the black singers.

Elvis listened on and, when he had the time, played on. He also played football. He played for the Humes High Tigers, and surprisingly was considered rather too small to make the top grade. But he was fast learning to stand up for himself and he'd hurl himself in where the action was, without stopping to consider whether he might get hurt.

Where, in earlier years, Elvis would think

Giving them all he's got at Fort Wayne, Indiana in March 1957

twice or thrice before saying boo to a goose, he was now gaining confidence all the time. He got in a few fights, almost always getting in the first blow, just to be on the safe side. Some of these fights were about the length of his hair, or the loud colours he preferred for his clothes.

The football coach insisted that he either cut his hair or be dropped from the team. Elvis told friends, 'I let my hair and my sideburns grow out just to make me look more like a truckdriver than a schoolkid. I hated being so young.'

Strangely, as his singing and guitar-playing improved, so he became more and more reluctant to perform in public. When high-school organizers put together the end-of-term concerts, most of them didn't even realize that Elvis could perform. In the end, he did agree to sing in one show. It was a very full production indeed, with nearly thirty acts involved. Normally encores were allowed, if called for, but the schedule was so tight that this particular year they were banned.

Just one act, the one student who did best, could return at the end of the show and perform 'one more time'. And it was Elvis, by a mile. He'd opened with a real weepie of a romantic ballad and unbiased observers insist that he moved most of the teachers to tears.

But what Elvis needed most of all was a job. Singing, he figured, was a part-time hobby. But he needed to work, simply because his parents were getting way behind with the payments on the apartment. The more he worried about the future, the further behind he got with his studies.

For a time he worked as an usher at Loews State Theater in downtown Memphis. He quite liked the job, even though it took up five hours every evening through the week, and only paid a grand total of thirteen dollars. In the end he had to quit because he just couldn't cope with his studies and his love of music. He also worked in a metal factory, starting after lunch and working through to near midnight, then snatching some sleep and getting to class on time.

This was no kind of life, he decided. His parents agreed, and forced him to give up the job – in fact, Gladys Presley went out to work again, as a hospital orderly, to keep some money coming in.

As Elvis has said, 'People work and they try to do the best for themselves, but sometimes it seems it just isn't worth it. There are ways you can be penalized just for being industrious and careful with your money.' What in fact happened was that the Presleys were evicted from their home. The reason was

that with Mrs Presley working, the total income was over the limits set by the local authorities for families housed in the apartment block.

Later they were allowed to return, but for Elvis it had been an eye-opening period. But he still worked when he could – mostly mowing lawns in the neighbourhood to earn money to see shows, buy records, have a night out at a local carnival.

As regards movie heroes, Elvis was a keen Tony Curtis fan, emulating as best he could the Curtis ducktail haircut. And when he finally came to leave Humes High, he'd majored in woodwork, history and English, and had been a willing, if erratic, member of the English, history and speech clubs.

Graduating was one thing. Finding a job which might suit him was another. So the summer of 1953 was, for Elvis and most of his classmates, a period of soul-searching. The majority went straight into a routine factory job – and Elvis started work for the Precision Tool Company in Memphis.

His next job was as a truck-driver for the Crown Electric Company, reckoning to earn maybe $40 a week. He was the newest and youngest on the staff roster, so he had to put up with a lot of jokes aimed at him, especially with his ever-lengthening hair and his one true companion, his guitar.

Nobody could see Elvis doing anything more than a mundane job. The trouble was that he was polite and helpful but he didn't look as if he had any fires of ambition burning inside him. He'd just get the job done, then go home, but to what? To his music, maybe a date with a local girl, maybe just a night listening to any one of ten radio stations.

But one afternoon in that summer something special was to happen. Elvis was meandering along Union Street in his beat-up old van when he espied the premises of the Memphis Recording Service. It's all part of the Sun Record Company, and the special service they provided was studio space so people could make happy birthday or anniversary discs for their nearest and dearest.

Elvis had a five-dollar bill burning a hole in the pocket of his patched-up trousers. He wanted to spend four of those hard-earned dollars making a two-sided birthday gift for his mother.

He took his guitar along. And he knew which songs he'd sing – 'My Happiness', a song written in 1933, before Elvis was born, and a 1950s hit first for the Ink Spots and later for Connie Francis. The B side was to be 'That's When Your Heartaches Begin', the kind of song guaranteed to reduce his old schoolteachers to sentimental tears.

A similar reaction came from Marion Keisker, who was the manager of the Memphis Recording Service. She felt that Elvis sang so beautifully that she ought to tape what he was doing separately and present it to Sam Phillips, boss of the Sun Record Company.

This was a stroke of genius. Sam Phillips had carved his business out of the mixed music of the area, and he loved black music best of all. A white man, he went for the basic rhythms of the black sound, but he realized that if he was to hit the big and richer white market he'd have to have that music performed by a white singer. With Elvis Presley he was to find success, with a blend of country music and rhythm and blues.

Phillips was a shrewd operator in many ways, but he was to prove a natural-born loser in others. He discovered top talent like Roy Orbison, Johnny Cash, Jerry Lee Lewis and, biggest of all, Elvis Presley. He was to give them all opening breaks in the pop music world. And he was to lose all of them to bigger concerns.

He'd been a disc jockey and he moved to Memphis when he became act-booker for the Peabody Hotel there. He found that the outstanding black musicians in the area could get on record only if West Coast companies bothered to cart their equipment over to the East Coast.

Being a good businessman, he set up his own studios, and concentrated on selling the Memphis-styled blues. He then sold the tapes to the big national companies. It was a money-making exercise, and he was both talent-spotter and ideas man.

Among the artists he recorded, prior to Elvis's first visit to the organization, were B. B. King, Bobby Bland, Junior Parker, Ike Turner and Howlin' Wolf. Presley appreciated all of them. From the studios Phillips set up his own label. Up-and-coming talent at professional level called in on him and he signed them, for a while anyway.

Elvis called in as a complete amateur, but once he'd demonstrated his vocal style, a whole lot of action was triggered off. His style immediately appealed to Phillips, who had repeatedly said, 'It would be worth a billion dollars to me to find a white guy who looked good and who sang in the black style.'

It was the kind of soul approach he wanted. Sam Phillips listened to the tape of Elvis wailing through 'My Happiness' and was reasonably impressed, though he felt there were a lot of rough edges to be smoothed down. He asked what the unpleasant sound in the background was, and it turned out to be Elvis's battered old guitar, which certainly had not recorded well. However, Elvis himself had registered well,

By 1957 Elvis was turning
away from stage shows to
the film studios

Rehearsing for a television performance

particularly with Marion Keisker who was quite amazed to see a young guy with such long sideburns.

It was not until a few days before Elvis's birthday in 1954, his nineteenth, that Sam Phillips and Elvis really got together. The meeting triggered off a few months of constant rehearsing, Elvis singing along with guitarist Scotty Moore and string bass expert Bill Black.

They worked together right through to mid-June of that year before the first records were made. Elvis had made a few more straight demo discs, notably 'I'll Never Stand In Your Way' and 'Casual Love', but this one was, hopefully, for real.

Marion Keisker had tried to get Elvis on record much earlier, but it was a song called 'Without You' that most appealed to Sam Phillips. That happened to be one of the few songs that Elvis just couldn't sing. He tried it every possible way, but it always sounded dreadful.

During the rehearsals and the actual sessions, Elvis tried country music, blues, straight ballads and intense religious songs, but the one that did the trick was 'That's All Right Mama', a song recorded for the specialist Bluebird label more than ten years before by Arthur Big Boy Crudup.

Having heard Elvis sing maybe 200 different songs, this was the one that got through to Sam Phillips and made him feel it was worth investing money in it.

He said later, 'This was the one that made the hair stand up on the back of my neck. It was magic. It just had to be a winner.'

THE first Elvis Presley record. 'That's All Right Mama'. hit a couldn't-care-less pop scene in August 1954. Though people with ears to hear knew from the start that it was an extra-special performance. with Elvis delivering a high-pitched and intensely urgent vocal. Sam Phillips didn't have the resources to give it adequate financial backing.

Pop was a crowded business even then. with record company executives determined to find something new to counter the non-activity of the mournful or chirpy ballad singers. Those who could spread the word about music liked the Presley approach. and he got more good reviews than sales early on. Phillips himself felt. 'It's such a mixture of white and black that they'll probably try to run us out of town when it gets heard.'

He knew that such musical barriers had not been broken before and that there was a general feeling they never should be.

How to get the record heard by the masses? Phillips took it along to the disc jockey. Dewey Phillips (no relation). who had a programme called 'Red Hot and Blue' on the local station WHBQ. In fact it was a station which traded in black artists. but Presley fitted that side of the scene more than the white. Elvis heard that the record was being played. but recalls he couldn't bring himself to listen in. So he took himself off to the cinema. leaving his parents alone to hear what was said about his performance.

The record was rapturously received by the listening public. Dewey Phillips played it as a one-off experiment. but fans started phoning in and demanding it be played again. The pressure on the station switchboard got heavier. Presley himself stayed in the comforting darkness of the cinema. and when he got home. there was a message delivered by hand saying that Dewey Phillips wanted to interview him . . . on the air.

Shaking with fear. Presley presented himself. He said instantly that he'd rather not do the broadcast. because he had never been interviewed before. didn't know anything at all about being interviewed and in any case didn't have anything to say. Dewey Phillips simply said. 'Shut up. sit down – and don't say anything dirty.'

While the records played. Dewey talked casually to Presley. He asked him about his childhood. where he went to school and how come he sounded so black. When the records ended. Phillips stood up and shook hands with Elvis and said a fast thank-you-and-goodbye.

When Elvis stammered that he thought he was going to be given the interview treatment. Phillips revealed that he'd had the microphone open all the time. so Elvis Presley was now known to thousands of people in the Memphis area.

DISC DEBUT

It was work as usual at the factory next day, but Elvis soon left to face his future in the pop music world. Scotty Moore and Bill Black had to cope with the demand for Presley's services and even broke up their own band, the Starlight Wranglers, just so they could work with him on stage.

'That's All Right Mama' hit the top of the Memphis area country charts. *Billboard* magazine, bible of the music business, said that Elvis Presley was 'a potent new chanter who can sock over a tune for either the country or the rhythm and blues markets'. And that was a first national paper write-up for the 'potent new chanter'.

appearances. During 1954 it seemed to him that honours were being poured upon him all the time. He had no idea, then, as he happily toured big local venues, just what a fearsome outcry his style of performance was going to cause.

He got on the radio programme 'Grand Ole Opry' in Nashville, Tennessee – a tremendous honour and generally reserved for long-established acts in the field. Elvis got established in about six minutes, or as long as it took to play both sides of his first record.

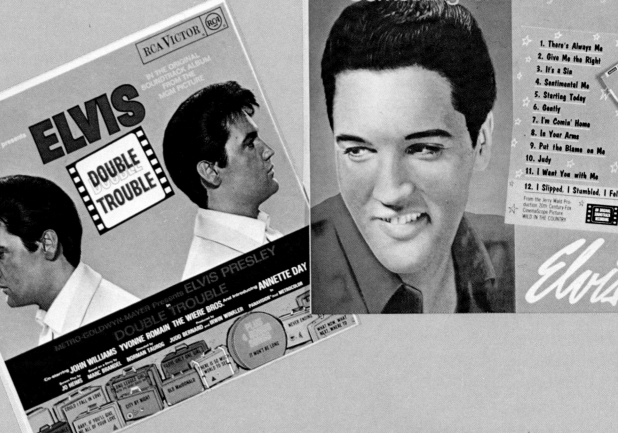

Elvis was to make a total of five singles for the Sun label – and good condition copies of any of them fetch prices of up to £100 these days. 'That's All Right Mama' was backed with 'Blue Moon of Kentucky', and the others were: 'Good Rockin' Tonight'/'I Don't Care If The Sun Don't Shine'; 'Milkcow Blues Boogie'/ 'You're A Heartbreaker'; 'Baby Let's Play House'/ 'I'm Left, You're Right, She's Gone'; and 'Mystery Train'/'I Forgot To Remember To Forget'.

Elvis started out making big-time personal

He also got on the 'Louisiana Hayride', which was broadcast from Shreveport.

Elvis didn't exactly cut a dashing figure. For a start he had severe acne, which did his face no good. His hair then was fairish-brownish, or just plain mousey, very long and well-greased. But he was six foot tall and well built.

He sang his up-tempo numbers and the hip-wriggling was to earn him the title of 'Elvis The Pelvis'. Drummer D. J. Fontana was soon to be added to the Moore–Black backing team, and Elvis was clearly building a name, particularly across the south.

His first really big public performance was at the Overton Park Shell in Memphis. New-found fans started screaming for him, and the atmosphere of excitement at the presence of a new star was remarkable. Elvis found it got through to his very bones, and he worked harder than he'd ever worked before. Every fibre of his being was involved in the selling of songs like 'I'll Never Let You Go Darling'.

He seemed to be here, there and everywhere. The Reverend Carl E. Elgena, pastor of a Baptist church in Des Moines, was to declare, 'Elvis Presley is morally insane.' And he didn't finish there. 'The spirit of Presleyism has taken down all bars and standards,' he thundered. 'Because of this man we are living in a day of jellyfish morality.'

But when the National Religious Broadcasters were informed at their convention in Washington, 'Elvis is one of the biggest problems we've got, a problem of American society,' the fans rallied even more to his support.

The speaker warned his audience, 'Much too many are going crazy about Presley. The better job

The act was frankly erotic. And the seeds were sown for what was to be one of the most violent anti-pop campaigns in the history of the music. Newspaper writers in the south started it, and by the time Elvis was signed to the huge RCA Victor record label and to manager Colonel Tom Parker, the whole campaign was in full flight. It's worth breaking the story line here to deal with the criticisms in full.

When Elvis really hit it big and got his name in the papers, along with pictures of his kiss-curl and his curled lip, he was inevitably copied by half the young population of the States.

you do in your field of religion, the sooner Presley will go.'

But Elvis didn't go.

Instead, churchmen in various parts of the country were further provoked to say what they thought about Elvis. One said:

He is simply the subconscious nature of modern youth in time of turmoil. We have been through the stages of the Charleston, the Big Apple and the swooning of fans over Mr Frank Sinatra.

I feel that the emotional nature of young people has produced Elvis Presley. Part of adolescence is change. We are living in a world where it is pretty hard for adults to remain emotionally stable.

That was the world of 1955–6.

There was a priest, Father Daniel Clement, from Memphis, who felt compelled to issue dire warnings to his flock. He said of the local boy who was making good, or bad, according to viewpoint, 'I advise both parents and children to stay away from Presley shows or

In certain areas, Elvis was instructed by local authorities to modify his act. He asked, respectfully, 'How in the peapickin' world can I help it if I go wild when I sing?'

Five teenage boys in Connecticut who were picked up on robbery charges said they had stolen to get money to go to New York to see an Elvis Presley show. Inevitably the prosecutor at their trial offered his view, 'Elvis Presley is an inspiration, clearly, for low IQ hoodlums, and ought to be entertaining them in the State Reformatory.'

And Elvis, thrust more and more into controversy, commented to a Memphis journalist

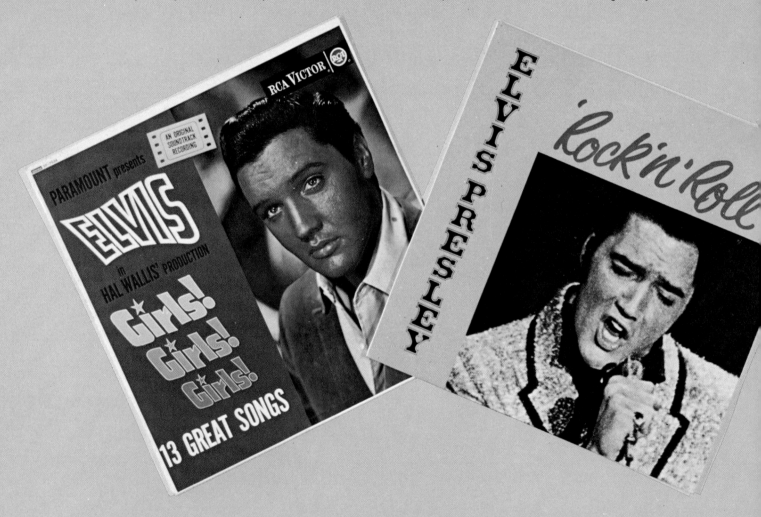

movies. The singer's morals may be above reproach. But he must be judged on how he entertains and how that entertainment affects those who are watching him.'

The cinemas and shows were packed out. Everywhere. The more violent the campaign against Presley, the stronger the reaction of the fans on his behalf. Sometimes Elvis played clubs where minors, those under 21, couldn't get in to see him. The fans often sought revenge by wrecking the place . . . from the outside.

simply, 'If I thought that was true, sir, I would quit and go back to driving a truck. I wouldn't do anything to hurt anybody, sir. Money doesn't mean anything to me. It's the business of singing that I love.'

In schools, colleges and universities the length and breadth of the States, principals were laying down laws. 'Get rid of those sideburns and that long hair or the only course open to me is to expel you.'

When the criticism got too heavy, Elvis would seek solace from his mother. Even in peak stardom, he always turned to her for advice.

'Do you think I'm vulgar in my act on stage, momma?'

'You're putting too much into your singing, though you're not vulgar. But keep up that kind of activity and you won't live to be thirty.'

'But, momma, I just can't help it when I sing. I have to jump around. And I sure don't feel sexy when I'm singing – if that was true, I'd be in one of those institutions where they send sex maniacs.'

Presley has no discernible singing ability. His specialty is rhythm songs that he renders in an undistinguished whine. His phrasing, if it can be called that, consists of the stereotyped variations that go with a beginner's aria in a bathtub.

For the ear he is an unutterable bore. Nothing as talented as Frank Sinatra in the latter's rather hysterical days at the Paramount Theater. Nor does he convey the emotional fury of a Johnnie Ray.

From watching this so-called new sensation, it is wholly evident that his skill lies in another direction. He is a rock 'n' roll variation on one of the most standard acts in show business: the virtuoso of the hootchy-kootchy.

Even the magazine *Down Beat* had it in for Elvis. 'He represents the nadir in American taste.'

Without planning it, Elvis Presley at the age of 21 was the most talked about singer in the world – in fact he was the most talked about citizen of the world.

The critics were divided on his ability. Those into the world of pop regarded him as a true original. Those who couldn't appreciate the nuances of different pop styles didn't rate him at all.

Jack Gould was television critic of the *New York Times*, a highly influential publication. He did not rate Presley when first he clapped eyes and ears on the singer.

A Las Vegas columnist said he was 'suffering from itchy underwear and hot shoes'. Someone else said he sounded like 'a lovesick outboard motor'.

All that, and characters who would meet him in the street or in a drug store and threaten to beat the daylights out of him simply because their wives/ girlfriends/sisters had taken a fancy to him.

Though the criticism was to die down eventually it built up steadily during the first couple of years when Elvis took himself and his sensationally sexy stage image around the south.

Before returning to just how his impact built up in the mid 1950s, it is perhaps worthwhile reproducing one of the reviews that Elvis found both hurtful and amusing. It was from *Time* magazine:

Is it a sausage? It is certainly smooth and damp-looking, but whoever heard of a 172-lb sausage, 6ft tall? Is it a Walt Disney goldfish?

As the belly dance gets wilder, a peculiar sound emerges. A rusty foghorn? A voice? Or merely a noise produced, like the voice of a cricket, by the violent stridulation of the legs?

Words come out, like raisins in a cornmeal mush. And then all at once everything stops, and a big trembly tender half smile, half sneer smears slowly across the CinemaScope screen.

But back to the formative years. Bob Neal, a disc jockey, managed Elvis's affairs for a while, but the second record was no smash, despite the publicity

It has the same sort of big, soft, beautiful eyes and long, curly lashes, but whoever heard of a goldfish with sideburns?

Is it a corpse? The face just hangs there, limp and white with its little drop-seat mouth, rather like Lord Byron in the wax museum.

But suddenly the figure comes to life. The lips part, the eyes half close, the clutched guitar begins to undulate back and forth in an uncomfortably suggestive manner. And wham! The midsection of the body jolts forward to bump and grind and beat out a low-down rhythm that takes its place from boogie and hillbilly, rock 'n' roll and something known only to Elvis and his Pelvis.

Presley was getting in the southern states. America was the land of so-called 'regional breakouts' – a record which hit in one part of the country sometimes led to full national recognition, but sometimes just stayed big in one region.

To get Elvis to the position where half the nation loved him and the other half reviled him needed somebody extra special on the management side.

Bob Neal certainly tried hard to find that extra-special something. He was pushing Elvis and

There were several 'elder statesmen' of the country field on the show, and both Slim Whitman and Faron Young were, years later, to become regulars in the pop charts. Presley was the young guy on the bill, and the undisputed star was Hank Snow. Snow had a production company going for him, and he'd appointed a man named Tom Parker to act as general manager.

For Elvis there were problems. First, he felt that on every stage-show performance he had, in a sense, to overwork to stay up there with all the established acts on the bill. Second, he had not exactly set the charts afire with his second and third singles from the Sun label, and he had a feeling he might yet prove a one-hit wonder.

Third, his style of performance was more into the wild excitement of the big-beat rhythm and blues field than the more sober moon-in-June approach of

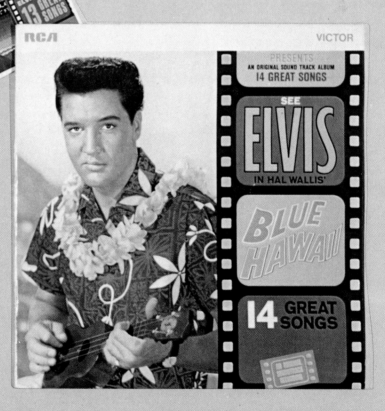

his group as hard as he could. He tried top networked programmes, including Arthur Godfrey's Talent Scouts television show, but it was a fruitless journey Elvis and his musicians made to New York. It was a case of 'hate at first sight' between the ebullient and dogmatic Godfrey and Presley, so for Presley it was back to the southern states for all-in package shows in the country-music field.

the country singers. It led to ructions after some performances. Many fans would react wildly to Elvis's wild act, then when he'd gone give rough receptions to some of the headlining acts who didn't put half as much energy into their work.

Elvis got involved in the show-biz razzamatazz. Buying a Cadillac was essential for any up-and-coming country star, and Elvis decided that pink was his colour. So a pink Cadillac it was – something worth photographing and something for the fans and the industry to talk about. And Tom Parker got involved with Elvis.

It was all rather cloak-and-dagger at first. Parker was a showman from way back. When he got into management, he took only top names – Eddy Arnold and Hank Snow, for example. But his grounding was in wheeling and dealing. He had a shrewd, instant-type attitude towards making a fast buck. One story concerns the way he was involved in running a sideshow in one of the big travelling fairs that moved all over the States. Business was rough. So he and his cohorts held a meeting and most of them decided that if the customers wouldn't come in at a price of 50 cents, then the best thing was to cut the admission rate to a quarter, 25 cents.

Parker wouldn't hear of it. He considered that it would be suicidal to cut the rate, and that instead it should be increased to a dollar-a-head admission. Naturally his friends assumed he'd gone stark staring mad.

But Parker hadn't finished telling them. 'We put the admission at one dollar but say that if anybody isn't satisfied we'll refund half the money.' A lot of people weren't satisfied but didn't like to raise the question of the refund. A lot of people asked for 50 cents back. But the point was that a lot of people did go in, and the very lowest anyone paid was the original 50 cents.

This was the man who helped present Elvis Presley on stage. He had noted just how big Presleymania was becoming. Because of his essential canniness he never let the singer know of his interest, but he was watching every development. While Bob Neal was able merely to do his best as a manager, the man who was to build the Presley saga to phenomenal status was hovering in the wings.

Long before he had a fully national hit record, Presley was a pop hero. He was being hailed as the King of Western Bop, and other writers called him the Hillbilly Cat. He was serving up his pop in the style of those old evangelical singers he'd seen in church. And the girls were screaming for him in a way that hadn't happened since Sinatra was at his peak.

Parker promoted him in a few more shows. One thing that did emerge was that other artists hated following Presley's act. He left his audiences in such a high state that it was impossible for anyone else to perform through the massed yells for encores and so on.

Gradually the fans started grabbing for Elvis. They were after his hair, his clothes, anything they could lay eager hands on. That fourth Sun label record hit the national charts, though only just. Since Parker was convinced that Elvis couldn't become truly big as long as he was with the Sun label, much of 1955 was spent not only countering the adverse stories created by Presley's stage act, but also planting stories that he would soon sing for a major label, which meant major promotion to go with the contract. The bidding that followed reached no astronomical heights, but then Elvis was still, at national level, an untried artist.

There was so much hassling that in the end the amazing Tom Parker, outspoken and teak-hard, though with an off-beat sense of humour, was empowered to work out a recording deal on behalf of Elvis. He went to RCA Victor on the strength of the say-so of an old friend, Steve Sholes, head of the artistic department of the company in Nashville.

This is where Sam Phillips bows out of a superstar story. It was a manoeuvre he was to repeat several times afterwards with other big artists. But what he got was $35,000 for the year left to run of Elvis's contract with Sun, plus a $5,000 fee to Elvis for signing. And, what's more, RCA took over all rights to Elvis's previously recorded material.

It was a sizeable deal for the time, but bore no relation to the incredible sums of money Elvis was to earn later on. Further deals were linked with the Hill and Range publishing company.

The seeds were well and truly sown. From a birthday present recording in a small studio in Memphis, Tennessee, Elvis was now to be given the big treatment. RCA were ready to spend a fortune launching the boy. Colonel Tom Parker, now very much in the driving seat, was prepared to sweat buckets to see Presleymania take off right round the world.

RCA's first move was to release several of the old Sun records, but to give them national publicity. This was to pay off in a really big way with the release of 'Heartbreak Hotel', early in 1956, the earthy, violent, vitriolic answer to all the soapy-soft pop that had been in vogue for years.

This was what was to make Elvis Presley a household name right round the world.

THE ROCK

'HEARTBREAK Hotel' was the clincher. Though there was a certain amount of reluctance in the UK to release a record by an unknown American white hillbilly, it did come out – and it hit Number Two spot in the charts in May 1956, spending a total of nineteen weeks in the Top Twenty. It was Number One in the States, having entered the charts there three months earlier.

And it was the start of a new era of music.

Colonel Tom Parker – the 'colonel' tag was an honorary one, but he insisted on using it – had pulled some remarkable strings to get his artist on networked television in the States. Once seen, of course, Elvis was never forgotten.

It was then the hate campaign started in earnest. He was burnt, in effigy, by the girls in a New York convent, for instance. And the Colonel was up to every move. As a personal protest against what he called narrow-minded interferers, he had Elvis do one television show singing as usual, but not moving a muscle. That took remarkable self-control on the part of Presley. And when Elvis finally received the accolade of an appearance on the Ed Sullivan television series, the cameras were instructed to focus on the top half of his body. This simple gesture was allegedly designed to prevent people being dismayed or outraged by the energy expended by Presley's torso.

What it really did, however, was get him talked about even more. Presley had his first Gold Disc award (for 'Heartbreak Hotel') in double-quick time, and he was to break sales figures and records every time he had a disc on release.

'Heartbreak Hotel' was written by Mae Boren Axton and Tommy Durden with a little help from Elvis himself. That was his contribution to the black rhythm and blues field; the flip side, 'I Was The One',

REVOLUTION

was written by Aaron Schroeder, Claude de Metrius, Hal Blair and Bill Peppers, and was into the country and western side of pop.

In that first year the hits flowed solidly and fast. In America, 'I Want You, I Need You, I Love You'/'My Baby Left Me' was the follow-up, written by lyricist Maurice Mysels and composer Ira Kosloff. This was recorded on 2 May 1956 – like 'Heartbreak Hotel', in Nashville.

Then came 'Don't Be Cruel', backed with 'Hound Dog' – both going 'gold' on strength of sales, though on the same record. He sold six million, and the record topped the charts in the States for eleven weeks. 'Don't Be Cruel' was written by Otis Blackwell and Elvis himself; 'Hound Dog' was by the remarkably consistent writing team of Jerry Leiber and Mike Stoller. It had been written some four years earlier, and was another highly charged mixture of musical styles.

Then came 'Love Me Tender'/'Anyway You Want Me'. 'Love Me Tender' topped the US charts for five weeks and became the first disc in history to have an advance sale of more than one million – in other words, it went 'gold' before it had even hit the record stores. This was written by Elvis Presley and Vera Matson, though was actually based on an old long-faded song 'Aura Lee', dating back some hundred years. The original was said to have been a favourite Civil War song. 'Anyway You Want Me' was by Aaron Schroeder again, but this time with Cliff Owens as partner.

Four giant hits in the first year of trading as E. Presley, international star.

In the UK in that first year, 1956, the order of release changed but he still had six Top Twenty titles – 'Heartbreak Hotel' (2), 'Blue Suede Shoes' (9), 'I Want You, I Need You, I Love You' (14), 'Hound Dog' (2), 'Blue Moon' (9), and 'Love Me Tender' (11).

All this happened while he continued to go out on tour, as a star in his own right now, and with tremendous support from Colonel Tom Parker, ideas-man *extraordinaire*.

When he played dates like the Dallas Cotton Bowl, the local authorities, worried about possible reaction from a crowd of nearly 30,000, erected a ten-foot fence between the stage and the auditorium. Presley, dressing more sharply than ever, arrived in a white convertible of extreme length. Predictably the crowd went wild. First with anticipation, and then with the realization that they were in the presence of someone very special.

While Elvis earned his oats on stage, the Colonel was raking in the money on souvenirs. For his boy, in well under a year of his management, was now the biggest thing in show business. The whole world wanted to see Elvis. But the Colonel had some ideas about that, too. There wasn't anything he could do about Elvis being on stage regularly in the States, since so many people had already seen him. There was no surprise element, then.

But the rest of the world, the Colonel decided, could wait. What Elvis would do would be to make movies. That way, it was argued, he could play to a million fans in just one night, whereas it would take him two whole years on the road to play to anything like that number of people. So, making films was the short cut to bringing happiness to the greatest number of fans.

Some of the more sceptical folk in show business figured there was another argument. By keeping people outside the States waiting in anticipation of a sometime-soon tour, they'd not think of straying from Elvis to some new up-and-coming pop performer. Besides, if he started appearing in London, Hamburg, Copenhagen and Paris there was a chance that he'd prove something of an anticlimax. He might just disappoint the fans by not being able to live up to the reams of fantastic publicity about him pouring forth across the Atlantic.

No, Elvis would stay put. He'd make records and films, and when he had to he'd go on the road in the States.

By April 1956, the movie career was on the way, with a screen test at Paramount, handled by Hal Wallis, a tough-nut producer who had made all kinds of films in a long career – from Martin and Lewis quickies to heavy dramas.

Elvis's test was easy enough. He played with a long-time actor named Frank Faylen, and won a three-film contract, each movie worth an increased amount of money.

The first film was *Love Me Tender*.

It was originally called *The Reno Brothers*, but was retitled to coincide (and cash in on) his single 'Love Me Tender'. It had Elvis as a country boy who falls in love with, and marries, his brother's girlfriend. But the brother, believed to have been killed in the Civil War, suddenly turns up out of the blue one day, to cause serious confusion. The film ended with audiences misty-eyed as Elvis died and his off-stage 'ghost' voice sings about him. A remarkable finale.

Most of the songs were of country origins, but the film did extend his acting talent a little. Elvis did not emerge as a classical actor, but his presence was

Only 'Loving You' showed Elvis
as wild on film as he was
on stage

Taking it like a man (left) in 'Jailhouse Rock'. (Above) 'Loving You'

undeniable: hair by now dyed jet black, flashing teeth
– flashing eyes, too.

It was a carefully planned movie debut. The
effect was less sensational in the States, where Elvis
had already been seen on television and on stage, but in
the rest of the world it was a first look at the man who
had the entire pop industry held by the scruff of the
neck.

That one was in black and white, the next was
in full colour. *Loving You* played an important part in
establishing Elvis Presley as one of the ten box-office
stars of 1957 in the movie world. He was beating some
of the long-established giants of the screen. And he

actors will help him out, and advise him, when
otherwise they might well be jealous of him.

This film was invaluable in projecting the
Elvis image, because it came nearest to showing him
as he really was (and is) on stage. In retrospect, it
seems that it might have been a better debut film
than *Love Me Tender*.

Now this hectic year for Elvis was further
stretched by his third movie. It was as if he'd stepped
on a production line there in Hollywood and couldn't
get off. The third film was *Jailhouse Rock*, which
threw up a hit which was Number One in the USA in
May 1957, and in the UK in January 1958. An EP

was being hailed as the new James Dean, in terms of
personality and image; or if not Dean, then certainly a
new, singing Marlon Brando.

Loving You had him playing Deke Rivers, a
lad with a great talent for singing rock and roll. The
blondely beautiful Lizbeth Scott was in this film and
she said afterwards:

There's no denying the sheer physical power
of this boy. At 21, he gives the impression he has
lived for forty years. He's no great natural actor,
but he gets by on the strength of sheer charm.
Besides he's so helpful on the set. He's a real nice
down-to-earth guy, and that's why a lot of other

of four titles from the movie was in the Top Twenty
at the same time.

Jailhouse Rock was tougher stuff by far. In
one scene Presley the convict is flogged by a sadistic
warder. Despite the character he played, the film
gained him even more sympathy. He starts out a real
toughie, but ends as a man who finds he has a soft centre.

By now Colonel Tom Parker had the whole
show-business world eating out of his hand. His 'boy'
was working harder than any other artist in the rock
field. When he did a live show, he had to have full-
scale police security. He even did a couple of weeks in a
richly paid season in Las Vegas, but that was no

Brooding and (right) pensive in 'Loving You'

sensational success. At this time, Elvis's position was as a hard-edged punk-rock singer, not as some pin-up figure for matrons and mums in the champagne and caviare circuit. That kind of prestige was to come much, much later.

If that was an error of judgment, then it was the only one to which Colonel Parker could plead guilty. Any time Elvis felt like arguing, the Colonel just poured out a few details from his personal brochure marked 'experience'. Sometimes it seemed that the Colonel must be a hundred years old, in view of the things he had packed into his life.

He was an old-style boss-figure. He insisted on having complete control over his artist. There was to be no split authority. The thing about the Colonel was

Swearing in – Memphis, 24 March

March, 1958 – Hollywood-style farewell

that he had been caught out before many times. Now it was his turn to insist, in the words of W. C. Fields, 'Never give a sucker an even break.'

This was the man who once had an act called 'Colonel Parker's Dancing Chickens'. They danced because they were standing on a hot plate, hidden by a thin layer of straw. It was easier to jump around than stand still and get burned. Meanwhile the music off-stage would be the old country number 'Turkey In The Straw'.

He was up to every trick in the book. He used simple psychology, too. He'd tip off disc jockeys and newspapers so that they were ahead of the field in anything Elvis was going to do. That way the maximum number of fans would turn up – the Colonel looking

suitably surprised as to how they happened to find out.

He made sure Elvis worked hard, but he also made sure he was happy. He gave him plenty of money to spend, but banked or invested the rest. Every deal he did was calculated to give the greatest possible advantage for the artist. As for the Colonel . . . well, it is said that he gets at least 25 per cent of everything Elvis makes, but the figure has been guessed at being substantially higher.

Elvis was involved in every kind of merchandising. He had his name attached to wristwatches, scarves, trousers, belts, magazines, pens, just about every possible kind of commodity. And the basic 'take' for Elvis and the Colonel would be around eight per cent of the retail price.

Tom Parker: 'Don't explain it, just sell it'

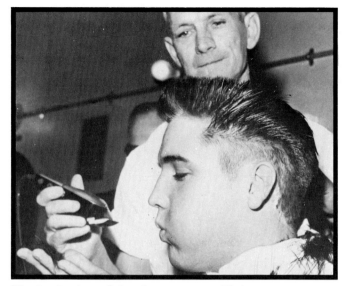

The beginning of the clean cut new Elvis

little matter that hadn't till then been considered.

Once the US Army decided it really did need Elvis, a very heavy security campaign was set in motion. For example when he reported, early in January 1957, at the Kennedy Veterans Hospital in Memphis for his medical check, he was the only would-be rookie on parade. The Army didn't want hassles with the newspapermen and television crews that were obviously going to be there. A year and a couple of months later he was inducted into the Army.

Throughout 1957, rumours had been circulating that Elvis would definitely get preferential treatment in the US Army: that he'd become a general entertainer, singing for his colleagues and that they wouldn't even cut his hair short. Naturally this led to a great deal of

In the middle of the activity Elvis returned to Tupelo for concerts. His mother was naturally delighted with the way her boy's career was going but sometimes she'd confide to friends that she looked forward most to the day when Elvis would retire and settle down and marry a nice girl. She was worried, she said, about the way some people were constantly running him down.

But when Elvis was making *Love Me Tender* both she and he had something else to worry about. It was a letter from the draft board in Memphis asking him questions about his home, his marital status and his health. Nothing to worry about, he was assured, just a general check-up.

However, the truth was that Elvis was liable for call-up like any other American boy and it was one

January 1960 – Squad Leader and Sergeant

resentment and not even the wily Colonel Parker could do much about avoiding the bad feeling.

All Elvis could do was make up his mind to work as hard as he could stockpiling films and records before he went in for his two years' conscription – and let the rumourmongers get on with their gossip.

He made the movie *King Creole*, filmed in black and white, and shot on location in New Orleans. Supporting cast included Walter Matthau, Carolyn Jones and Dean Jagger, and the eventual soundtrack album was one of the finest he has ever made. Titles: 'Trouble'; 'Crawfish'; 'King Creole'; 'As Long As I Have You'; 'Hard-Headed Woman'; 'Dixieland Rock'; 'Don't Ask Me Why'; 'Lover Doll'; 'Young Dreams'; 'Steadfast, Loyal and True'; and 'New Orleans'.

The ideal soldier

Elvis played a young lad named Danny Fisher, mixed up in an area of hoodlums, night clubs, chicks and excellent songs. It was a realistic sort of drama, with Elvis doing well on both rock and ballad songs.

By the time he went into the Army, he'd already had twelve Number One records in the States, and each album had been a hit. Elvis said, '*King Creole* gave me the chance for the first time to play somebody other than Elvis Presley. But I can assure you good folk that I'm not just going to play at being a soldier.'

He had had a deferment on his enlistment date, simply because the Paramount film studios stood to lose at least $350,000 if Elvis had been unable to complete *King Creole.* So it was that he reported to the Memphis Draft Board offices at 6.30 a.m. on 20 March.

Many people foresaw the beginning of the end for Presley. They figured that he'd been a kind of rocking revolutionary who wouldn't be able to settle down to Army life and would probably end up doing a highly personal jailhouse rock. Others believed that two years was too long for a pop hero to survive without being available to promote his talent. He would, they predicted, be forgotten.

But in fact there were already signs of an almost deliberate change in Elvis's character. The evidence was in some of his records, and in the movie *King Creole*, towards the end of the story.

Elvis had started out as an untamed rocker. Two years on he seemed to be veering away from that out-and-out rock situation. He was more the Hollywood actor with a kind of all-family image. He was a singer who could tackle a hymn, or a romantic ballad, and still throw in a rocker to please the younger fans.

Maybe that was it: he'd planned a kind of escape route from what was supposed to be a short-lived future in rock and roll. The spell in the Army would in a sense be useful in letting him live down his fiery beginnings.

Though there was logic in this theory, and Elvis had proved the wide range of his appeal through 1957, it was a smack in the teeth for those who saw Elvis in the role of a rocking revolutionary, an anti-establishment figurehead.

Getting Elvis into the Army was no easy matter. Though the deferment granted was really a normal thing for men in all kinds of business who had urgent work to do, the anti-Presley brigade believed he had pulled strings for sordid financial reasons. 'My boy received no such treatment,' wrote one mother. 'It's indecent that you should let this monster Presley make the entire Army do as he wants.'

It was surely inevitable that Colonel Parker should be at the official induction ceremony – bearing balloons advertising the forthcoming *King Creole* movie.

But Elvis took the whole thing in a mood of super-cool. He was asked if he was frightened that some of the tough master-sergeants might have it in for him because of his superstar status. 'If they do, it won't be because of anything I do to provoke it. I'm going in to be a soldier and the Army can do anything it wants with me and send me any place.'

And on the day itself he said he would be having his hair cut off and yes, he was grateful to the fans who had written demanding that he be excused Army service so he could entertain his loyal following. 'But I have a duty to do and I'm gonna do it,' he said.

Then he was off to the Kennedy Hospital induction station by motorcoach, and it seemed that the whole press world was there. One telegram arrived which was read to a laughing Elvis, 'Release Elvis Presley immediately. It's unfair – you didn't put Beethoven into the Army.'

There was no answer to that.

And there was a message later from the Governor of Tennessee, Elvis's home state, 'You have shown that you are an American citizen first, a Tennessee volunteer, and a young man willing to serve his country when called upon to do so.'

So it was that Elvis, and a bemused gaggle of other recruits, left for Fort Chaffee. He'd arrived early that morning as Elvis Presley, controversial pop superstar and Hollywood box-office buster. He left as Private Presley, E., US Army number 53310761.

He didn't have anything to worry about, financially speaking. True, his Army pay was only around $80 a month, and that wouldn't buy him many off-duty flash clothes, but he had other sources of income. He might lose out on personal appearance fees, but there was a basic $1,000 a week from his record company, plus monies from his publishing interests, the merchandising, and the income from box-office receipts on the four movies he'd completed.

But to the credit of Elvis and the surprise of his critics, he refused to trade in on his status. He didn't even mention the fact that the US Government stood to lose at least half a million dollars a year in income tax all the time he was in the Army.

At Fort Chaffee there were the usual complaints about Elvis's special treatment. For instance, a press conference was called, and the critics presumed it had cost the Army and therefore had cost the taxpayers. One newspaper snorted, in an editorial, 'One rubber-legged, hirsute, adenoidal guitar-twanger gets drafted into the Army and instead of letting him fade into well-deserved obscurity, the Army public relations officer takes special pains to assure full publicity.'

Like the other soldiers he was given $7 in cash to tide him over to payday. He was asked what he planned to do with it and he said with a grin, 'Probably start a loan company.' In fact, he had to pay out 65 cents of it to get a haircut. Virtually all his hair vanished under the clippers. It was then ceremoniously burned, along with other rookie hair – just to thwart fans who might pester the Army headquarters with requests for locks.

That it was all some kind of circus, simply because of the demands of the press and reporters, wasn't Elvis's fault. And in no time he was getting high compliments from those who commanded him. One top sergeant, 'I don't much like his music, but I wouldn't mind being first sergeant of a company of his calibre of men.'

There just had to be a song to commemorate the induction and there was. It was by the Three Teens and called 'Dear 53310761'. 'Marchin' Elvis' was another.

For all the fooling around, there was no denying that Elvis was beginning to be accepted as a good guy, not bad, by a large proportion of the adult population. He'd had his hair cut, which for them was tantamount to having been brainwashed, and he was obviously settling into a very good soldier.

The publicity the Army sought on him, and got on him, did no harm for future recruitment either. When he left Fort Chaffee after initial training, one Colonel Connell handed out a statement which read:

I never expected this. He turned out to be an honest and forthright young man. My impression of what he was certainly changed as soon as he came here. He had to put up with a lot of things, in terms of publicity and ribbing from his mates, and most of us would have found it hard to take. But he's leaving us with a good wholesome feeling.

And it couldn't have been easy for Elvis. Not with tough, grizzled old soldiers inquiring daily whether Elvis was missing his 'teddy bear' – or asking solicitously about all those chicks who were constantly throwing themselves at him.

The early months in the Army passed easily enough, however, because Elvis was so determined to gain a good image for the rock and roll industry . . . to prove that those in it could put their shoulders to the wheel as well as those in any other walk of life.

But though he was off the pop-record scene in person, his image never left it. The singles and albums were released as usual – his *Elvis Golden Records* was a huge seller, and the first in what was to be an unbroken run of in-Army singles, 'Wear My Ring Around Your Neck', came out.

And there was the *King Creole* movie. While Elvis learned to slave over a hot tank, the critics were at last giving him credit for his acting ability.

But tragedy within the Presley family was just around the corner. In August 1958, Elvis's mother fell ill. For a while she'd struggled on, despite feeling drained of energy most of the time, and she tried hard not to show Elvis, when he visited on leave, just how painful life was.

The doctors in Memphis diagnosed hepatitis, and a very serious case of it. Elvis was summoned from his Army camp in Texas and for two days and nights took it in turns with his father to maintain a bedside vigil in the Methodist Hospital there. Vernon Presley was in the private room when she finally gave up the struggle for life. Elvis was asleep at Graceland, the family home he always regarded as a memorial to his beloved mother. His mother died of a heart attack, 14 August 1958.

The inscription on the tombstone reads, 'She was the sunshine of our home.'

The story is that Elvis, numbed with shock and only too happy to tell journalists that he'd always been very much a mother's boy, wanted to hold the funeral at Graceland, the estate thrown open to visitors . . . 'because mama loved my fans and they have the right to say a last farewell to her.'

But it was decided not to go ahead with the plan. Even so, 3,000 people turned up to represent the Tennessee public, along with 400 family mourners, for the service at which a Gospel group, the Blackwood

(Right) Keeping fit with Uncle Sam

Brothers, sang 'Rock Of Ages'.

As a superstar in the pop firmament, Elvis had one basic problem. Deep down he was shy and often lonely. When he had problems, he invariably turned to his mother – and it is said that he never let a single day go by without telephoning her. That she was only 42 when she died seemed to Elvis to be the most heart-breaking aspect of the whole tragedy.

One of the last things said by Gladys Presley was a request that, if anything should happen to her, Elvis and his dad would always stick together. And as Elvis prepared to go to Germany as part of the replacement crew for the Third Armored Regiment, plans were made for Vernon Presley to go along as well.

On 19 September, Elvis and hundreds of other US soldiers left by ship for Europe, from the Military Ocean Terminal in Brooklyn. Naturally Colonel Parker was there, and naturally he laid on as much show-biz razzamatazz as he could. For instance, Elvis gave a final press conference, and from it came an EP record 'Elvis Sails', which was to sail its way into the bestsellers.

Though he'd been a popular soldier during his stay at Fort Hood, the authorities there were glad to get rid of him – for some 15,000 fan letters poured through the Army mail depot every single week he was there.

But as he sailed, there were many in the music business who felt he would never be able to make a return to the industry he had so dominated. Many felt that rock and roll was only a short-lived craze. Others felt that a year or so out of the country would mean Elvis would become a forgotten man. They reckoned without the shrewd planning of the illustrious Colonel Parker.

At the tail end of 1958, Elvis hit Number Four in the charts with 'One Night'. Early in 1959 he was up top with 'A Fool Such As I', and 'A Big Hunk O' Love' was a chart-topper in the summer of that year. Albums, too moved straight into the bestsellers. And stories of how he was proving a really good soldier were fed back from Germany to keep the image moving along.

That final press conference was full of quips, but also moments of seriousness. Of his mother he said, 'Apart from being a real friend, she was my advisor. She'd always try to slow me up if ever I thought I wanted to get married. She was right – it helped my career not to get married.'

He said one of the first things he wanted to do in Europe, if he was anywhere near France, was to look up Brigitte Bardot in Paris. He never got around to that.

As the troop ship, the *General Randall*, arrived in German waters, there was a great deal of interest

among the locals. For Elvis was already a very big name there, and many of the homegrown singers had copied his style. Which was to prove embarrassing for them when the 'real thing' arrived in their midst.

Elvis took the reception from nearly 1,000 screaming fans on the dockside in Bremerhaven in his stride.

In Germany, his main duties were to be to drive a jeep. His father and grandfather arrived and stayed in a luxury hotel for a while as they looked around for a suitable house in which to live for the duration of Elvis's service.

Though he received no special favours from the Army authorities, Elvis was allowed to live off the camp – he was chauffeured to the base every day in a luxury limousine.

And the fan letters kept pouring in. Some, just addressed to Elvis, US Army, found their way through. It was estimated that his postbag was 10,000 letters a week. Then there were the people constantly ringing him from the States – fans, well-wishers, parents of other soldiers.

Elvis was not able to wander round the neighbourhood because there were fans everywhere, waiting to talk to him, and who maybe would just try to tear him to bits.

If life was healthily active for Elvis, then it was certainly active for Colonel Parker, too. Despite the hit records, he had to use other means to keep the Presley name before the public. He talked of big schemes to relaunch Elvis once the Army days were over. And when Elvis had a spell in an Army hospital, suffering from inflamed tonsils there was the opportunity for publicity in the will-he-won't-he-sing-again controversy that raged.

The RCA Victor people were constantly hitting headlines about how Elvis's popularity hadn't slumped one little bit during his absence – and produced sales figures to prove it.

There was news about his next movie, to be shot as soon as he got out of uniform . . . except he'd go straight back into uniform again to make *GI Blues*. The storyline was, surprise of surprises, about a tank sergeant in the US army, based in Germany. There had already been a few songs about Elvis's khaki-clad days, and they'd sold well.

Some of the fulsome statements from his Army officers about his highly disciplined Army days were calculated to be headlined, too. Like the words of one commandant:

He's fooled us all. We had our stomach full to here of these celebrities, singers and actors, and we

**1 March 1960, Berg, on demob day.
Plans to write his Army memoirs
never materialized**

49

The modest house Elvis lived in in Germany and
(above) his luxurious Memphis home

figured Presley for just another lightweight. But
he's never angled himself into anything easy and
he shows exceptionally good judgment for a kid
worth a few million dollars. This guy Elvis has
made it popular to be a good soldier. It's great
for us.

And in one American magazine, a question
which sent a shiver up and down the spinal columns of
Hollywood moguls, and Colonel Parker, was posed:
'We've got plenty of hillbilly singers and actors of
your talent, Elvis, but how many good soldiers do we
have now that General MacArthur is retired and
General Eisenhower is in the White House? Since you
have done so well in the Army and show so much
liking for the military life, why not re-enlist and make
it a career?'

There is a story that Colonel Parker had a
dummy front page of a paper, headlined 'Elvis To

Re-Enlist', wrapped it round the regular paper and had it delivered to movie producer Hal Wallis, who stood to make a fortune out of films when Elvis came marching home.

As Elvis neared the end of his service life, he found himself commanding a three-man reconnaissance team in the 32nd Scout Platoon.

One radio station in America hailed his homecoming as 'a musical, cultural and military phenomenon'.

In the midst of all the praise for the good soldier Presley, there were those who believed his clean conduct sheet would contribute to his eventual ruination. Presley wasn't a goodie – not in terms of the way he sang, or the way he looked, or the way he rocked and rolled on stage. Guys like Pat Boone, clean-cut and crew-cut, were the goodies. Elvis was anti-establishment; the others were instantly rated as ideal husband material.

Many thought that it would have suited Elvis's image more for him to fight the Army's regimented approach to life – to strike out as an individualist. In other words, he'd have been easier for fans to identify with if he'd really gone out to buck the system.

So it was believed that Elvis had once again done it all wrong. Each commendation from a straight-guy Army officer was, it was argued, another nail in the Presley coffin.

And if the real Elvis was suffering from a bad attack of image change – for the worse, because it was 'better' – then there were imitators galore prepared to copy his style and play the anti-establishment role with relish.

But once out of the Army, Elvis was to follow the dictates of his heart and do something else reckoned to be drastically wrong. Like . . . getting married.

THE HERO RETURNS

CERTAINLY it was a much-changed Elvis who left the US Army. On 5 March 1960, he was officially a civilian again. But the sideburns had gone, so had most of his hair, and he seemed to have calmed down in many ways. No longer was he wearing the old-style outrageous clothes, though the love of pink Cadillacs was still burning strong within him.

But he got straight to work. The first post-Army single was 'Stuck On You', which hit the Number One spot in the US and was Number Two in Britain. No problems, then, about whether he was still the top boy in the beat business.

All the same, Elvis was nursing a secret. He'd met a girl, a dark-haired beauty in Germany. She was the daughter of a US Air Force officer, and she had tremendous personality and charm, even though she was only fourteen when he first set eyes on her at a party. Towards the end of his stay in the Army, the couple had dated quite a few times.

And without his mother to talk him round when marriage entered his thoughts, Elvis found himself thinking about the future. And often he felt the future just had to include the dark-haired Priscilla Beaulieu.

But in the early 1960s it was regarded as near-suicidal for a pop star to get married – or, if he was married, to admit to it. The idea was that the star had to be somehow larger than life – but at the same time attainable. In old Hollywood movies, the girl fan sometimes did get to marry the leader of the band. If fan did meet star, then there had to be at least a chance they'd fall in love, get married, and live happily ever after. A wife was clearly a barrier. The pop-scene thinking was that anybody who got married was finished as a star. He had put himself completely out of reach. There was another girl . . . so the fans would move on to some new guy who didn't have a girl.

Elvis had been out of the Army just a couple of years when a four-headed eight-handed challenge rose to test his staying power at the top of the pops: a group called the Beatles.

Having learned their trade the hard way, in the smoky and noisy clubs in Hamburg, the Liverpool group introduced a new word to the rock scene: Merseybeat . . . the original Liverpool sound. Where, for years, it had been almost one-way traffic in pop across the Atlantic, from America to Britain, the Beatles were to change everything around.

Suddenly Britain and British groups ruled the roost. As had happened with Elvis there were myriad groups trying to copy the original, and the United States threw up a lot of them. But the Beatles were to challenge even Elvis's remarkable record-selling career.

And then came the news that one Beatle, John Lennon, was – whisper it – he was married. His blonde wife, Cynthia, a childhood sweetheart, was for many months kept out of the way. She and John had a son, Julian, but the family side was taboo.

Elvis Presley, working harder than ever in the States, knew the problems caused by stars suddenly getting married and thus putting themselves out of reach of their fans. He noted the controversy when in the end John Lennon decided to admit he had been married quite a while.

There were stories that Elvis was secretly married – but then he was dragged into any rumours on any subject. He wasn't married, but he was thinking about it. And he was thinking especially about that girl named Priscilla.

Elvis coped with most of his problems himself, though he was also protected from most of them. He had plenty of highly-paid advisers who coped with things, made decisions for him, stopped him from worrying by doing the worrying themselves.

The films flowed thick and fast. After *GI Blues* it was *Flaming Star*, then *Wild In The Country*, both for 20th Century-Fox.

The *Flaming Star* epic had him as a halfbreed, hurled into a series of mental anguishes because of his mixed blood; an outsider figure, essentially a loner, it was a part which provided Presley the actor with some testing moments. He came through it well.

Then, the week his father married Dee Elliott, whom he'd met in Germany around the same time as Elvis first met Priscilla Beaulieu, he brought out a smash single 'It's Now Or Never', based on the operatic aria 'O Sole Mio'. It seemed to give further evidence that Elvis was moving away from rock and roll – into the all-round entertainer class. This huge hit was originally written in 1901, with lyrics by the Italian G. Capurra, music by Eduardo Di Capua. But new words were cooked up by the team of Aaron Schroeder and W. Gold. Global sales were reckoned at 20 million and it topped the charts just about everywhere.

It was followed up by 'Are You Lonesome Tonight', another oldie – dating back to 1926 when it was written by Roy Turk and Lou Handman.

The movie *GI Blues* threw up a million-selling album, the soundtrack featuring the following songs: 'Tonight Is So Right For Love', 'What's She Really Like', 'Frankfurt Special', 'Wooden Heart', 'GI Blues', 'Pocketful of Rainbows', 'Shoppin' Around', 'Big Boots', 'Didja Ever', 'Blue Suede Shoes' and 'Doin'

The Best I Can'.

Two million copies of the album were sold. And 'Wooden Heart' was taken out as a single – and was to be Elvis's 31st gold record. This song was written by four different people – Fred Wise, Ben Weisman, Kay Twomey and Bert Kaempfert – but in fact was an adaptation of an old German folk song, originally entitled 'Muss I' Denn Zum Städtele 'Naus'.

Strangely enough, the bandleader Bert Kaempfert was around to produce the Beatles for the first time on record . . . though they were in the German studios just as a backing group for guitarist-singer Tony Sheridan.

And back on the movie side, where Elvis was making an average of three full films a year, his acting success in *Flaming Star* was repeated with *Wild In The Country*, which was to be his last for 20th Century. Later he was to switch between Paramount, United Artists and MGM.

Wild In The Country had him once again in the familiar rebellious, outsider-looking-in situation. The story wasn't up to much, despite having originated with Clifford Odets, an established writer. Elvis played the part of a budding writer who couldn't stay out of situations of violence. He had some simmering, shimmering scenes with Tuesday Weld, and Hope Lange was cast as a social worker trying to help the young 'outcast'. All in all it worked a few more wonders for Elvis Presley's Hollywood status.

On record again, Elvis showed his talent for singing hymns and religious songs – the album *His Hand In Mine* was another triumphant success.

It really seemed, for a while, as hit record followed big-money movie, that Elvis could do no wrong. In Nashville he was invited before the Tennessee State Legislature, where the elected representatives thanked him warmly for bringing so much fame to the area.

And yet there still seemed something wrong with the way Elvis was running his career – or the way in which the Colonel was running it for him. As a battle campaign it was relying more and more on just the twin-pronged approach of records and films.

The singles certainly flowed through 1961: 'Surrender', 'Wild In The Country'/'Feel So Bad', 'His Latest Flame', 'Rocka Hula Baby'/'Can't Help Falling In Love With You', 'Good Luck Charm', which took him into 1962, and was followed by hits like 'She's

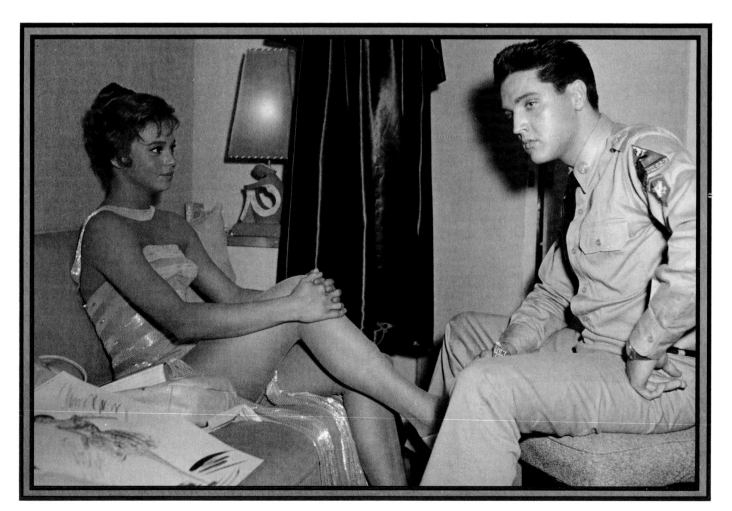

Backstage with Juliet Prowse and (right) on the set of 'G.I. Blues'

'Viva Las Vegas'

Not You 'Return To Sender', and in 1963 'One Broken Heart For Sale', 'Devil In Disguise', 'Bossa Nova Baby Kiss Me Quick'.

The Beatles were ruling the group-scene roost by 1964 when Elvis had 'Viva Las Vegas', 'Kissin' Cousins', 'Such A Night', 'Ain't Loving You Baby' and 'Blue Christmas'. And Beatlemania was by no means abating through 1965 when Elvis hits included 'Do The Clam', 'Crying In The Chapel', 'Tell Me Why', 'Love Letters'.

He did occasional personal appearances in the early 1960s, but there were many who figured that he had more or less decided to go into hiding, with visits only to the studios or the movie set. It was argued that the Beatles and the whole group business was too big to fight and that Elvis should maybe go partly into retirement and hope it would all go away.

Certainly one or two of his records made only slow progress to the top of the charts. Some, like 'One Broken Heart For Sale', had to be pushed quite ruthlessly even to show in the Top Twenty. Elvis was still one of the highest-paid performers in the world, but just for a change he had a real fight on his hands. Apart from the Beatles, there were many other groups regularly hitting the top spot in the charts.

In Britain, for example, the groups included the Shadows, Gerry and the Pacemakers, the Searchers, Billy J. Kramer and the Dakotas, Brian Poole and the Tremeloes, the Dave Clark Five, the Four Pennies, the Animals, the Kinks, Herman's Hermits, the Moody Blues, the Seekers – and bigger than all but the Beatles, the Rolling Stones. Most of these groups weren't even formed when Elvis first emerged.

There was no evidence that the hard core of Elvis fans were put out by the changes going on, but viewed from outside it did seem that Presley was being guided along a money-making course which didn't give a great deal to the fans.

The argument was always used that by making a film Elvis could show himself to millions in just a month or so, whereas if he went out on tour he could play to only a comparative handful of fans. He didn't like flying, and that was another understandable reason for his reticence to get out on the road.

But the fans didn't blame Elvis for his stay-at-home tactics. They blamed Colonel Parker for 'misleading our boy' – and his shoulders were certainly broad enough to bear the weight of the criticism.

Elvis, basically, was making a film, then bringing out a soundtrack album of the music, then making another film. After *Wild In The Country* came *Blue Hawaii*. This was in 1961. He did a show in Hawaii and that was it for eight years. He did no more 'live' shows. Not until the Beatles had effectively stopped as a unit did Elvis show himself again on stage.

It's been said that the death of his mother led to him becoming listless and disinterested. But it seems more likely that the Colonel simply didn't want him to tour, even to places where he was constantly hero-worshipped, like Britain, because there was a danger that he would prove an anticlimax.

The argument went:

He's a good performer. But his loyal fans have been kept waiting so long, they would expect a super-human performance from him. And the British press would hammer him anyway because of his earlier reluctance to tour. Putting it plain and simple, he's dead scared to show himself lest the real thing doesn't live up to the carefully packaged image.

As for the Colonel – well, his aim was simply to make the most money for his one-and-only artist-client. He knew little about the artistic side and it is said he usually didn't bother to read the script of an Elvis film, preferring to wait for the première. Certainly, from *Blue Hawaii* onwards the quality and performance value of Presley movies deteriorated.

Blue Hawaii had him in spectacular scenic

'Flaming Star' offered Elvis one of his most demanding roles

One film fast followed another: left, 'Girls Girls Girls',
bottom left, 'Charro', below, with Ann-Margret in
'Viva Las Vegas', right, with Ursula Andress in
'Fun in Acapulco'

58

locations, baring his chest, and singing ersatz ballads of love. *Follow That Dream* came along, with him portraying a country hick and, in terms of comedy content, very good indeed. Next it was *Kid Galahad* for United Artists, where he had to take part in some tough fight scenes. He was a charter-boat skipper in *Girls! Girls! Girls!*, which had a fair song content and was filmed again in Hawaii.

Elvis must have known that his movies were slumping at the box office through the mid-1960s, but he still left everything to the Colonel. Both grew rich on the guaranteed fees for the movies, and the record royalties were still very high – because fans outside America, starved of anything much from Presley, bought everything that was released. Though Elvis must have read the reviews, and been told about the receipts which had been dwindling for a few years, he

was basically protected from the business side of life. He was usually holed up in his various homes, working in the studios, watching movies all night, and he was surrounded by his friends-cum-bodyguards, known to all and sundry as the Memphis Mafia.

Though Elvis was said to have been involved with dozens of girls, some of them actresses, little came through in the way of hard factual details. He fooled around with his high-powered motorcycles, played football to keep in good physical condition and every so often he went on a serious diet to lose weight. He always did have a weakness for hamburgers and ice cream – and, indeed, his mother had always had a weight problem.

He wasn't exactly a prisoner in his own home, but it just wasn't easy for him to get out and about any more. So exactly how many girls he dated isn't known. Many of those who have earned good money by writing about their dates with Elvis and the Memphis Mafia have dealt more with fiction than fact.

But in the back of his mind was always . . . the now strikingly beautiful Priscilla Beaulieu. And 1967 was to be the year when they got married – Elvis's murmured 'I do' causing a mass heart-flutter round the world.

Through the 1960s, Priscilla's name had been mentioned in the context of Elvis Presley, but nobody really forecast marriage. She had expressive grey eyes, hair which was really dark red, but which photographed black. She grew up in Memphis but had spent time in Germany with her US service officer father.

She went to high school there in Wiesbaden and started going to parties in Germany, apparently just one of a group of girls who went together. Elvis was to say later:

She was just a kid – more than ten years younger than me, but she wasn't like so many of the other girls. I guess most of 'em were a little overawed by me, by what I'm supposed to be. Dunno why, because I'm shy myself and do my best to make other people feel at ease. But with this chick it was different. She didn't give the impression she was in any way tongue-tied.

When Elvis returned to the States, he still wrote to Priscilla and after she had returned to America with her family, she often stayed at the Presley home. When they finally announced that they were getting married on 1 May 1967, the news spread round the world like a forest fire – through radio, television and ticker tapes. This was it. The number one eligible bachelor was taking the plunge, Elvis going personally to collect the licence, costing fifteen dollars, from the

Clark County registrar.

It didn't take Colonel Parker long to get things organized on behalf of his 'boy'. The press were there, with clicking cameras, and the Colonel stage-managed things for the ceremony which started early in the morning. It was to last less than ten minutes, with the word 'obey' being left out of the commitment clause.

There were about 100 guests, including newspapermen, at the wedding breakfast. It was a magnificent meal – including fresh salmon, oysters, fried chicken and gallons of champagne.

The music included 'Love Me Tender', which had long been a favourite of Priscilla. And afterwards the couple left for a four-day honeymoon. It couldn't last longer, because Elvis was still filming.

Elvis was living still in Graceland, but he had also bought a large ranch in Mississippi, where he had horses, cows and farming equipment. He called the Ranch Circle G – the initial of his beloved mother. But the first real married abode for the Presleys was a vast, rambling house on a mountain side in Trousdale, one of the high-living areas of southern California. A house with a magnificent view of the area, and a place where the security was so good that even Elvis Presley could find a little uninterrupted peace and quiet there.

Elvis was sought out for interviews, mostly about how it felt to be married at long last. He said:

Priscilla is something really special. There have been, in the past, girls I have liked better than other girls, but I never before fell completely in love with any one girl.

But I've always looked basically for qualities of love and sincerity and trust. There was a girl, when I was starting out as a singer. Maybe she didn't take me seriously, but as soon as I started touring, she upped and married another guy. That broke my heart . . .

In fact it made me wary of ever being so hurt again. I felt for that girl the way my father felt for my mother when they first met. I know that to be true, because I talked to my dad about it.

Suzannah Leigh, blonde British actress, filmed with Elvis in *Paradise Hawaiian Style*, and was specially interested when Elvis finally did get married. She said:

He is one of the most courteous and professional young stars I have ever met. True, he asked me out on a date – he wanted to go motorcycling – and I had to turn him down. But had I gone, I would never tell people what went on.

A man so charming is entitled to happiness outside his work. And he deserves his privacy. He has lived in a sort of goldfish bowl for years and years. When I worked with him I talked a little about marriage. And there was no doubt in my mind that Elvis would, one day, make a wonderful and attentive husband. Equally there was no doubt that he would not rush into marriage just for the sake of it.

Soon after marrying Priscilla, Elvis was back at work – the film was *Speedway*. The film started production in June. By July Elvis was telling the world that Priscilla was going to have a baby – 'We really hadn't planned for one this early, but it seems to me that this is what marriage is all about.'

Those closest to Elvis believe that marriage and pending parenthood really gave Elvis his will-to-win back again. For there is no argument that his career really picked up from that point on – not, instantly, in financial terms, but in doing worthwhile things on records and in the movie studios.

The baby, Lisa Marie, weighing 6lb 15 ounces, was born in the Baptist Memorial Hospital, Memphis, on 1 February 1968. Statisticians pointed to the fact that it was nine months, to the very day, since Elvis and Priscilla were married. Priscilla stayed in hospital for several days, while Elvis tidied up things generally in Graceland.

So now the Presleys felt they were a complete unit. Once the excitement of the new baby had faded a little, Elvis started on the *Live A Little Love A Little* movie, a film which had him cast as a glamour photographer.

If there was a problem, then it related entirely to his Memphis Mafia. For they were not so necessary now. Elvis had his wife and baby. He didn't need, certainly to the same extent, the comradeship of the lads who had earlier spent so much time with him.

That there was a so-called Memphis Mafia at all was the brainchild of Colonel Parker. The various members were old friends, from the same neck of the woods as Elvis, and apart from comradeship they were there to do useful jobs. Though one – a former top footballer, Alan Fortas – would have the job of being in charge of Elvis's travel arrangements and the others all had specific tasks, their main job was to keep Elvis occupied during his off-duty hours.

They'd play touch football with him, or pool, or they'd provide entertaining comments when he laid on his late-night movie shows at Graceland. Red West was an important member of the group, an old school-mate of Elvis, and a former US Marine. He was a key figure in Presley's karate training sessions, and was

A stylish wedding – but a short-lived marriage. Opposite, Priscilla Presley after the break-up

also a very good musician.

It was a constantly changing team. Some decided they had to make a name for themselves without being in the 'shadow' of Elvis. One or two fell out with the bossman, or with his manager. Others just moved on for no real reason.

Talk to 'Mafia' men today, even those who left way back, and they all attest to the remarkable generosity of Elvis. He'd buy twelve high-powered motorcycles, to give one to each of the guys on his team. Some handled his clothes, his wardrobe, others would handle the hotel reservations. He treated all of them with honesty and used to say, 'They are all members of the Corporation of which I am the head. But even if they work for me, they are still all my friends.'

So they all went to his parties. They all helped in the entertaining. It was a weird sort of mass relationship. The only time there were harsh words was when a football game got a little out of hand. Elvis liked to win. He didn't expect any favours, but he still liked to be on the victorious team.

Most people understood that Elvis Presley was not like other people, and therefore he had to create his own lifestyle. He couldn't wander around window-shopping, or sip a malted milk in the local drugstore.

But he retained his old interests – like eating hamburgers, or playing the jukebox, or watching movies. The only difference was that he'd have it all brought to his own home. That way he could live in his old lifestyle, not having to play the international superstar . . . and get a little privacy.

He knew that out in the big wide world there were a lot of people he just could never trust. In his Memphis Mafia there were friends. Only friends.

But when Priscilla came on the scene, the Mafia scene had to change. Later, when there were the first glimmerings of trouble in the Presleys' marriage, Priscilla was to call the 'Mafia men' all kinds of names . . . notably 'goons, who stick to Elvis like so many burrs'. And there was no doubt that the long-time 'Mafia' men felt that Priscilla was an intruder. Elvis had loyalty for his old friends and love for his wife – but in the end one had to give way to the other.

He has never called his gang by the 'Memphis Mafia' title. He just calls them buddies, or chums. He admits that he has made few new friends since he first made hit records back in the 1950s. He also asserts that he's never needed new friends, because the old ones have so much loyalty for him.

As Elvis said in one interview, 'My boys are nearly all about my own age. They don't earn a fortune, but they do collect enough. We never have any fights about money. Most of them are from Memphis. We have the same roots, the same blood, the same emotions, the same heritage and traditions, and I find it a great comfort to have people around me who are like precious pieces of furniture from my own boyhood home.'

So Priscilla was put in the unfortunate position of getting married to a living legend and then finding she had come between her husband and his old friends. They had sustained him for so long that they resented her.

Ironically, when the marriage eventually fell apart, Elvis was immediately welcomed back into the fold by his old friends – his buddies. And his attitude was one of gratitude to them, with no sign of the obvious fact that he was the boss and could employ anybody he wanted.

But by the time Elvis had done it all wrong again – that is by testing his popularity by taking the 'drastic step' of getting married – he quite definitely was no longer regarded as a show-biz public enemy number one. Elvis Presley, husband and father, was in his own way a complete pillar of the establishment.

VIVA LAS

VEGAS!

LAS Vegas is one of the plushest, richest, flashiest places in the world. It's also the big gambling centre of the world. The top stars like to go there, because the luxury hotels there vie with each other to pay the biggest money for the biggest names.

Yet, the story goes, when Elvis Presley was booked into Vegas on one gig, the Colonel insisted on money in advance. He reasoned, 'They have an atom bomb testing place out there in the desert. If somebody pushes the wrong button, what happens to our fee?'

It's hard to know whether this was intended as a joke but the Colonel definitely wasn't joking when he charged $250,000 for Elvis to give one show at the Seattle World Fair. Nor was he smiling when he insisted on a special 'rain clause' in the contract, so that if it did rain on this huge open-air arena, Elvis Presley Promotions had the sole rights to sell their plastic umbrellas and raincoats.

His money-conscious manner has also emerged when various British and European promoters try to tempt him into letting Elvis appear abroad. One offered £150,000 for a single show – say $300,000. Said the jocular Colonel, 'Right, that settles my share of the money. Now let's talk about Elvis's fee.'

Someone else hit on a brainwave which he felt sure would appeal to the Colonel. The idea: to hire Wembley Stadium, home of many international sporting events. Put on Elvis in the centre of the playing pitch. The crowd for cup finals there is 100,000 strong, so Elvis would surely draw that number.

One problem: those high up on the terraces, or in the stands would hardly be able to make out Elvis's features. The lip-curling would pass unnoticed. The solution: put Elvis in a kind of glass bowl, only made of magnifying glass, so that he would be enlarged by something like nine times his normal size. Those in the front would get an extra-special view, and therefore pay extra-special prices. Those at the back could at least be sure of seeing Elvis's facial movements. But the story goes that when the idea was relayed to Colonel Parker, he said, 'If the customers are gonna get Elvis nine times bigger than lifesize, then the fee will have to be nine times bigger than lifesize.'

And that was the end of another effort to get Elvis Presley out of America for live shows, and more frustration for promoters who knew that as a performer, few could touch Elvis, let alone better him. Nobody could entirely understand the reluctance for him to show himself.

Instead films poured forth, with Elvis the pretty-good guy who sings for kicks and gets involved in routine situations. Box-office figures showed that the crowds were staying away – but even then his real fans in farflung parts of the world stuck by him.

'It's all Colonel Parker's fault – and anyway Elvis says that though he's too busy right now he will for sure come and play concert dates for us soon.'

And they were still saying the same thing ten years further on.

It Happened At The World's Fair was the first of the 1963 batch of films, with Elvis as a pilot whose big vocal moment was singing 'One Broken Heart For Sale'. Then he became a trapeze artist in *Fun In Acapulco*, featuring the usual attractive parade of girls. And *Love In Las Vegas* kept him up with his three-films-a-year schedule: in it he played a racing driver.

Kissin' Cousins had him in a double role, one fair haired and the other dark, otherwise indistinguishable . . . and undistinguished. *Roustabout* led him into 1964, at the very height of Beatlemania, when they topped the charts with 'I Want To Hold Your Hand', 'Can't Buy Me Love' and 'She Loves You', with 'Please Please Me' hitting Number Three spot and 'Twist and Shout' going to Number Two. Everything they released that year was a smash hit in the States.

But for Elvis things were not so good. 'Kissin' Cousins' was a single, but reached only Number Twelve in the charts. 'What'd I Say', 'Such A Night', 'Ask Me' – all missed the Top Ten though they were in the Top Twenty. For Elvis Presley, eight years a star by then, anything that didn't make Number One could be rated a flop.

Roustabout had him as a singer with a travelling carnival show. *Girl Happy*, also for Paramount, cast him as a night club entertainer. The producer of that movie was Joe Pasternak, whose son was to become top European disc jockey Emperor Rosko, and one of the greatest Elvis Presley fans in the business. Also in 1964 was *Tickle Me*, in which he was a rodeo rider, and there were a lot of curvy girls on hand – and also a lot of very bad reviews from the critics.

The films came out so fast and regularly that no factory production line could have improved the service. *California Holiday, Easy Come Easy Go, Double Trouble, Clambake, Speedway, Stay Away Joe, Live A Little Love A Little, Charro, The Trouble With Girls and How To Get Into It, Change Of Habit.*

When Elvis played Las Vegas for the first time in 1956, it was a misbegotten engagement. He just didn't fit. He was young, maybe over-exciting as a performer for the bejewelled matrons who made up much of the audience – and, as a 21-year-old new boy, he didn't know

how to cope. He worked the only way he knew, which was raunchy, rocking and raucous.

But by the time he'd got into the marriage scene, and really got himself together mentally so that live performances suddenly seemed a good idea again, he was ready for Las Vegas. And it was to prove equally true that Las Vegas was ready for him. This was 1969.

He'd gained new feelings about his status in the business through a television special he made for NBC. The show was made in midsummer 1968, shown to the American audience in time for Christmas and had a booking in Britain too, on the BBC-2 network.

People loved it. People also said it was a bit dated, but it was Elvis doing his own thing, and it was fascinating for new fans who'd never seen him in this kind of setting – as himself, and not in some hammed-up movie role — and for those who loved to wallow in nostalgia as they recalled first hearing him singing 'Heartbreak Hotel' and other classics he had made his own.

He had also been in the studios and cut some tremendous, musically satisfying tracks, with Chips Moman, a top producer. A couple of albums emerged, notably *Elvis In Memphis*, which was followed by *Back in Memphis*. In The Ghetto, generally accepted as one of his all-time great performances, and 'Suspicious Minds' also came out of those sessions.

So marriage, responsibility and a cautiously tested acceptance had put the man they'd long called 'King' right back in the mood to occupy his throne again.

Elvis was to star at the International Hotel, some thirteen years after he's first been in the Vegas area. It's not hard to believe Elvis's own confession that he was frightened half to death. Here was a man who had long been a legend in his own lifetime, but who hadn't appeared on a stage for eight years. He was also in a place where not all his memories were happy ones. A lot of reputations were at stake on the booking, not least that of Presley himself.

For the month he was to collect well over half a million dollars. He did an hour's act including twenty songs, and 'That's All Right Mama', the song that really started off the whole multi-million dollar industry called Elvis Presley, was amongst them.

He worked energetically, enthusiastically and above all brilliantly. This was the Presley of earlier days. Marriage, his fans said, was doing him a lot of good. The three-girl group, the Sweet Inspirations, were outstanding back-up singers, and it really did add up to one of the great 'comebacks' of all time.

It wasn't that Elvis had really been away . . . just that he'd been hiding a most important part of his talent from public view. It seemed obvious to everybody on that sensational opening night that Elvis just had to keep on working.

He said at a press conference, 'I'm really glad to be back in front of a live audience. I don't think I've ever been more excited than I was tonight.' And he added, 'Sometimes when I walk into a room at home and see all those gold records hanging around the walls, I think they must belong to another person. Not me. I just can't believe that it's me.'

It was, quite simply, one of the greatest historic moments in pop history, that International Hotel opening night. The songs flowed, most providing memories of great days clearly not yet past, but with some new songs, too: 'Blue Suede Shoes', 'I Got A Woman', 'That's All Right Mama', 'Love Me Tender', 'Can't Help Falling In Love With You', 'Yesterday' (out of the Beatles' songbook), and the new 'Suspicious Minds', which was to become his 51st million-selling single. He included 'I Can't Stop Loving You', one of the top songs in Ray Charles's stage act, and there was 'Johnny B. Goode'.

It was to be the start of a series of visits to the plushness of Las Vegas, though later he was to produce more of a cabaret act, featuring songs like 'Bridge Over Troubled Water' and 'Release Me', and rather less of the out-and-out rockers which marked that return after years in the wilderness.

Later, too, Elvis was to turn to making jokes about his own past. The older folk who made up the typical Vegas audience loved that. Some, ten years before, even fifteen years before, had worried about the effect Presley hip-swinging might have on their impressionable kids.

Now there he was, doing it all over again, but with a smile on his face and laughter in his eyes, and he says, 'There, see that movement? – they wanted to send me to prison for that.' And during that first season there were matronly ladies flinging up articles of underwear for Elvis to touch. At the end of each show there were fans trying to clamber up on to the stage just to get near him. They were used to all the big names in Las Vegas. But Elvis was poles apart from the normal, polite, gently-swinging acts in the Sammy Davis Jr, Frank Sinatra, Dean Martin category.

Albert Hand, a short bespectacled man from Nottingham, would not at first sight seem a typical Elvis Presley fan. But he really organized things for Presley's image in the UK. He ran the official Presley monthly magazine – it is still going, though Albert Hand died a few years ago. He was advisory president of the Official Elvis Presley Fan Club of Great Britain and the Commonwealth, and founder of the International Elvis Presley Appreciation Society.

As Elvis started that triumphant comeback campaign in 1969, then aged 34, Albert Hand wrote:

Pop singers have come and gone by the hundreds in the fifteen years Elvis has been at the top. Some we may still remember but vaguely; some we may not remember at all – not even for their one or two hit discs.

A very few – and it is a FEW – we may still remember because they are still round and about on the scene. But really, how few. Despite all the laudatory comments which launched them originally as 'the greatest' or 'the star of tomorrow and the day after', and other similar splurges that are tagged on to the releases of practically every new recording artiste.

The reason of course is that in the main those artists just have not been artists. Plainly not good enough. The other side of the coin is that the great big public is very fickle. Some recording artists of the past fifteen years have been very good, with high talent. But perhaps the magnetism of that talent was not powerful enough to retain fan interest.

But Elvis Presley: fifteen years later, nearly 30 films later, over 100 Gold Discs later, over 150 million sales later, is still with us, still very much the international star. Still wearing so firmly that Crown as King.

It is time that the infamous firm called Knockers Unlimited went into voluntary liquidation. It really is inconceivable that any level-headed person can find the integrity and sincerity to knock an Institution of fifteen years' undiminished popularity and achievement.

Admittedly some people may not like Elvis, nor find him to their taste. But surely they can appreciate that the King must have something in order to have maintained his crown for such a long period.

It is one thing to not find an artist to your personal liking. But quite another to knock and denigrate undoubted talent just for spite.

Though Albert Hand had passed on by then, those same knockers were predicting doom for Elvis even as he celebrated his 40th birthday with yet another hit record.

At 35, Elvis made another string of hits, most of them recorded in this fresh-as-new-paint state of mind he'd discovered. They included 'Suspicious Minds', 'In The Ghetto', 'Don't Cry Daddy', 'The Wonder Of You', 'I've Lost You', and on to 'You Don't Have To Say You Love Me' and 'There Goes My Everything' which gave 1971 a great start with two Top Tenners in the UK.

And 1973 also produced big UK hits to match the US performances – they included 'Until It's Time For You To Go' and 'American Trilogy', followed by 'Burning Love'. And the main ones in 1974 were 'Always On My Mind' and 'Fool'.

One particularly interesting point was that when

'Heartbreak Hotel' was reissued in Britain in 1971, it hit the Top Ten all over again.

A single shows something like three minutes of effort, while an album is a much greater test of an artist's achievement at any particular period. His albums in the years after the Las Vegas return-to-mania included *From Elvis In Memphis*; *The Elvis NBC-TV Special*, a double-album; another two-record pack called *Memphis To Vegas/Vegas To Memphis*; the brilliant *On Stage '70* album, which included that smash hit single 'The Wonder Of You'; *That's The Way It Is*; *Love Letters From Elvis*; *Elvis Now*, and two more double albums, *Elvis at Madison Square Garden* and *Elvis from Hawaii*.

At all levels, all the doubts about whether Elvis Presley could fight back against the years when he showed himself only on celluloid had gone. He hit the road again, looking fit and healthy and slim, and he did all the major cities in the States. But how about Britain? 'Elvis is booked steady for two years ahead, but maybe then . . .'

It was the same old stock answer. Nobody ever explained how he got booked up so far ahead when he, apparently, wanted nothing better than to visit Britain.

Elvis came near to knocking himself out as he roared round the States in his private jet. Few people ever got to see him, except on stage. It was from the airport to the hotel in a dark-windowed limousine, and a straight smuggling job up to the penthouse suite. Waiters and maids rarely saw him, and he demanded and got both peace and security.

Then into another limousine to go to the show. On stage, people did get to see him, set off in a brilliantly lit and presented performance. Afterwards he was off again.

He's been called 'the most remote star in the business'. And yet the handful of people from his worldwide fan clubs who have met him are instantly impressed by three things: the first, his instant friendliness and warmth; the second, the fact that he is incredibly handsome; and the third, his politeness and courtesy, be it to waitress or princess.

He has survived so many changes in the musical world. Each time he altered his style it was said he'd lose contact with his original fans, but instead they changed along with him. Pop music itself has changed many times since he spearheaded the rock and roll invasion.

There was the Beatle-inspired group era, then the heavier rock, then a stab at flower power and gentleness and peace, with groups like the Monkees turning out deliberately contrived teenybop fodder, then the progressives who virtually turned their backs on the audiences and played complicated music for their own personal gratification, and then on to out-and-out party rock as performed by the Slades of this world, and then it was teenybop all over again.

When Elvis celebrated his 40th birthday, on 8 January 1975, the world's newspapers gave the event a great deal of coverage. As always with such a controversial figure, there were two sides to the story. Some tried to paint a picture of a flabby hasbeen struggling to keep going in the young man's world of pop music; others gave genuinely warm tributes to a superstar who outlived and outfought all his contemporaries.

Much was made of the apparently 'unreal' life he had led right from the time he started making hit records. It was that which led to his divorce from Priscilla just three years before he hit the 40 mark. It would be wrong, however, to apportion blame for the breakdown of their marriage. The couple had little chance to spend time together, simply because of the extra action in Presley's own career. The birth of baby Lisa had kept Priscilla occupied, too.

But certainly the divorce settlement cost Elvis a lot. Reports suggest he settled property worth around £600,000 on her, plus alimony of more than £3,000 a month for his ex-wife and his daughter. And then, as his career moved ahead, though not without problems, close friends said he missed Priscilla more than anyone else in his life.

But Priscilla herself has said the problem was that she virtually became a show-business widow. 'We really hardly saw each other and when we did there were all his other pals around. Things did change a lot when Lisa arrived, but they changed back again when he left our home in Hollywood to work in Las Vegas.' In other words, the biggest triumph in recent Presley history was to be a major problem in his marriage.

Possibly Elvis never really lost those feelings about his mother, for he said:

Any girl in my life would find it hard because she'd have to live up to the standards of my mom. The proudest day of my life was when I gave her a pink Cadillac. It was a silly sort of thing. But she and I knew what it meant – that all the bad years were over. That Cadillac is still parked in Graceland. It's a sort of memorial to her.

For Elvis, in so many ways, being 40 was difficult. There were stories that he had become almost paranoid about security and that in strange hotels, he'd have somebody taste his food because he was

system endures, so will he.

And even if now at 40 he's a bit paunchy, depressed and uncharacteristically irritable, there is no doubt that anywhere in the world audiences will queue and fight and bribe to pay £30 for a lobster dinner to see, hear and adore him.

Ray Connolly, long-time Elvis addict and screenwriter of rock-inspired movies like *Stardust*, wrote in the London *Sunday People*:

Elvis has spent almost half of his lifetime so far as the world's biggest superstar.

For Elvis, being an adult has meant being one of the most famous people in the world. As a child he knew nothing but the poverty and deprivation

afraid of being poisoned.

Certainly there were problems about his weight. Sometimes his face sort of 'blew up' to give a mishapen appearance. And when the podginess was not on his face then it was around his waist. Elvis has, through the years, taken the greatest care over his personal appearance. He has worn deep-tan make-up if there has been the slightest blemish on his face. And his hair, originally fair and flowing, is still regularly dyed jet black, because black suits the moodiness of the man.

As for fears regarding his safety, he has long appreciated that political extremists, or kidnapping crooks after a fast million, could do a lot worse than use Elvis Presley as a hostage. British artist David Bowie, who arrived in the pop super league some ten years after Elvis, has long held the view that one day, somewhere, a pop star is going to be killed up there on stage through the action of some murderous maniac. He fears it could be him.

Elvis at 40, with no sign of his popularity diminishing, is a very wealthy man. He says, over and over, 'I rely absolutely on the Colonel. He's never let me do the wrong thing. Colonel Parker manages my career, my daddy invests my money and I mind my own business. You can't go beyond your limitations.'

So, as the *Daily Mail* said by way of tribute in London:

He is now an historic institution and global resource. Everything he does is surrounded by an air of mythology and as long as the uncontrolled and irrational adulation that is the basis of the star

common to families known as the White Trash of the American Deep South. As an adult he has known nothing but sumptuous wealth, adoration and fawning sycophancy.

At 40, Elvis looked pretty much the same as he did at 30 except for the bouts of illness which played havoc with his appearance. In the month that he celebrated that 40th birthday, he went into the Baptist Hospital, Memphis, where his mother had died years earlier, and the official bulletin said that he was suffering from fatigue and from a twisted colon.

Naturally there were rumours that it was something more serious still. Liver trouble was diagnosed by far-off 'experts' while other genuine doctors felt that the problem was caused more by his poor sleeping and eating habits.

Presley had, for years, found it hard to get to sleep at night. He'd lay on film shows, with the James Bond movie *Goldfinger* a particular favourite, and insist that his 'Mafia mates' sat up with him. Rather than worry about a properly cooked meal, he'd organize hamburgers and Cokes. In Elvis's case, alcohol couldn't be blamed for any illness since he's only ever been an occasional drinker, more often than not ignoring the 'happy juice' completely.

When, in March 1975, Elvis made his first public appearance in some six months, he told a packed audience at the Las Vegas Hilton, 'You should have seen me a month ago. I looked like Mama Cass.'

And he was saying that he'd have to lose at least 20 lb before he could go back on stage. And that decision might mean a diet based on yoghourt, or just clear soup, or possibly plain milk.

That Elvis, even at his age, manages to keep so much of his private life to himself is little short of a miracle. Tom Diskin is Colonel Parker's right-hand man and he has said, 'I hear these rumours about this and that in Elvis's private life. I just pay no heed. He's entitled to live his own life the way he wants and it's not for his management figures to try to interfere.'

But through his career the Presley image has been plagued with rumours. Every big pop star suffers, but if you are the biggest of them all then the rumours get that much bigger. A rumour can start in someone's front room, spread through a whole village and end up

virtually confirmed, in black and white, headlined, in the newspapers.

There have been many rumours that Elvis has died – mostly in a car crash. Someone thinks he saw Elvis drive through a town, then hears of a car smash somewhere around. He tells a reporter. The reporter rings the police, 'Any truth in the story that Elvis Presley has been killed in a car crash?' Maybe then somebody gets on to his management . . .

But the damage is done.

When Buddy Holly, who also started with Elvis in the mid '50s, died in a plane crash, there were many who believed the rumour that he hadn't actually perished but was so badly disfigured that he was living a life of meditation in a monastery on some way-off hilltop.

When Elvis Presley has taken a few days off, just for peace and relaxation, there have been stories that he's been dreadfully disfigured in, say, a crash, that the plastic surgeons are working on him, and that nobody will admit the story is true because the fans would only get upset.

Elvis has been hard-hit by the rumourmongers, to the extent that denials have been issued. But some rumours are planted, deliberately, by show-business contemporaries. They'll say, with a knowing wink, that Elvis is going to quit because his voice is permanently damaged, or that he is retiring because he's made his pile and couldn't care less any more about the fans.

Through the years the worst rumours, from Elvis's point of view, have been concerning his prospects of making a world tour. Somebody, maybe a hopeful agent or promoter, says that he's got just the right offer to get Presley to England, or Australia or wherever. 'It's on – one hundred per cent on.'

So the fans get excited. So eventually the story gets through to the Elvis management, who have to discount the whole idea – because the agent hasn't even got around to posing the offer.

But the fans don't know the background. To them, it is a case of Elvis building up their hopes, then dashing them at the last moment. Or of him chickening out of what they believed was a firm contractual deal.

Though Elvis, by the very nature of the way he has lived out his life as a superstar, is protected from much of the nasty side of show business, quite a few of the things he reads about himself give him great concern.

And it is no wonder that he sometimes worries about matters of security. He never was able to move around under his own steam, for fear of being mobbed. But is it not possible that some gun-crazed lunatic might just take a pot-shot at him one day?

IN terms of longevity, Cliff Richard, British top-popper comes near to rivalling Elvis Presley. Both dark-haired, both capable of singing virtually all kinds of songs, both genuinely and deeply religious.

Cliff Richard came through in late 1958, with a chart-topper of a single called 'Move It'. Elvis Presley's 'Heartbreak Hotel' had hit the British chart just a couple of years before. Cliff Richard was an immediate, fully paid-up member of the Elvis Presley fan club. He's always admitted it.

The television series *Oh Boy* was one of the most successful on pop music ever presented from London, and the producer, Jack Good, had a lot of faith in the new, but untried, Cliff Richard. So they met to talk about how Good would introduce Richard on his show.

He said, 'Cliff, on the show you can sing

IN HIS

FOOTSTEPS

"Move It", but you're not going to play guitar.'

Cliff said that he'd never done a show without it, wouldn't know what to do with his hands and anyway Elvis Presley always went on stage toting a guitar.

Good repeated there would be no guitar. 'And your sideburns must go. I want them shaved off.'

Cliff was astounded. It had taken time and patience to get the sideburns just right in the Presley style. 'No, please, anything else, but not the sideburns.'

Good said, 'They have to go. What are you trying to do? Just be a copy of Elvis Presley? Both the guitar and the sideburns go or you don't go on the show.'

And Cliff admits, to this day, that the decision was right. 'The time had finally come for me to give up looking like a carbon copy of my idol, Elvis. I had to prove to the fans that I was a chap named Cliff Richard, capable of being a personality in my own right – not just following in the master's shadow.'

But bits of the Presley image remained. Cliff Richard today is the epitome of respectability but there was a time when he attracted adverse criticism for the hip-swinging style he adopted in his act – just as Elvis had done in early days, when he was shot only from the waist upwards.

The trade paper, *New Musical Express*, commented on Cliff's television debut:

Producer Jack Good must be held responsible for permitting the most crude exhibitionism ever

(Left) Cliff Richard in the early 'sixties

(Above) P. J. Proby and friends

seen on British television by Cliff Richard.

His violent hip-swinging during an obvious attempt to copy Elvis Presley was revolting – hardly the kind of performance any parent could wish their children to witness. If we are to believe that Cliff Richard was acting 'naturally' then consideration for medical treatment may be advisable before it is too late.

While firmly believing Cliff Richard can enjoy a lengthy musical career, it can only be accomplished by dispensing with short-sighted vulgar tactics.

And at the time Cliff Richard said, 'Elvis and me, we're different – yet both of us lead decent normal lives. Elvis's army career showed him to be an ordinary guy who could mix well with his mates, who wasn't big-headed and was happy and willing to lead a life without special privileges.'

But in those days there were literally hundreds of young singers who dyed their hair black, practised the pout and the sneer, and rehearsed how to swivel hips as suggestively as possible. It was then that the joke about any of them started: 'He's trying to wear out his trousers – from the inside.'

John Lennon, and the other Beatles come to that, was heavily influenced in music by what Presley had been doing in the States. He said in his book *Lennon Remembers*:

In the early days in England all the groups were like Elvis and a backing group. And the Beatles deliberately didn't move like Elvis, that was our policy. But what I wanted more than anything else was to be bigger than Elvis – for the Beatles to be that bit bigger.

Perhaps they were just that, in the 1960s. But they were to split, go solo, and find success that much harder to sustain. The group disbanded at the time when Elvis was really finding his feet again.

Eric Clapton has long been a hero figure in the progressive rock field – posters proclaiming 'Clapton Is God' were splashed round New York. But he says of Elvis:

Discount the commercial rubbish he has done often during his career.

I just like to think of his trail-blazing glorious best, when he sang black man's music in white style, and taught the world something about true originality. He's still a hero of mine. You don't forget the early influences.

And Joe Cocker, also very much in the progressive blues field, admitted to borrowing presentation ideas from Presley. He says, 'Blues means black – that's what they say. But give Presley a good blues number and he sells it just right. You don't think of him as being white or black, both or neither. You just think of him as being . . . Elvis Presley.'

To Billy Fury, at one stage one of the finest of British rockers, Elvis was a hero figure – and Fury was to meet Presley for a short, but historic, summit chat one day in Hollywood.

Tom Jones was also much influenced by Presley – and when the Welshman also became a regular in the Las Vegas nightspots, he became a close friend of Presley.

John Barry is now a fine composer, with many movie-score awards to his credit, but early on he led his own band, known as the John Barry Seven, and he toured in the rock and roll shows which peppered the theatre-cinema circuit in Britain. Barry then played trumpet, although not notably well, but his group backed some of the big names.

He says:

I used to watch all these hundreds of performers who did their best to steal anything they could from Elvis. Really they had it made, because early on we didn't see much of the original Elvis. That was one of his own problems, created by not touring Britain. Had he toured the world at that time, he'd have put all the imitators to shame.

There's always been a lot of copying, idea-stealing in pop music, but nobody has ever matched Elvis for the sheer power of his rock and roll. I have respect in music for the original. And Elvis was, quite clearly, an original.

P. J. Proby, an American eccentric who had a short but hectic career, arrived in London to claim friendship with Presley – and quite certainly to copy many of his vocal mannerisms.

The names of big-star devotees of the Presley touch could go on for ever. The actual recording technique used was important. Elvis addicts will recall a falsetto sound on an early Presley disc, 'Party'. And will also recall that it was to be used by the Beatles later in 'She Loves You'. And the use of echo, which added so much to 'Heartbreak Hotel', was to be used by just about everybody in the business later on.

In the book *The Sound of Our Times*, Dave Laing wrote:

Presley's stage act was the model for rock singers who followed. His stage movements were prefigured by black performers on the edge of the rhythm and blues field, but he learned some of his stage movements from Bo Diddley.

To begin with it was what the rock singers did as much as what they sang that alienated older

people from them. For younger people, his act was an incitement to action. The action for audiences was dancing. If they were stopped from dancing, then there was just violence of some kind – seat-ripping, or just violence.

One of the big new names to emerge in 1975, when Elvis was 40, was Bruce Springsteen – launched into the big time with the dubious compliment that if he wasn't exactly the new Elvis Presley then he certainly was the new Bob Dylan.

Now Springsteen was only nine years old when he was turned on to pop music. He says 'I was inspired entirely by Elvis Presley. Anybody who sees Elvis Presley and doesn't want to be like Elvis Presley has to have something wrong with him. My hands were too small for me to wrap them round a guitar to give out "Hound Dog" when I was that young, but I tried again when I was fourteen and I've never stopped trying since.'

There are fan clubs honouring Elvis scattered right round the world. But some of the biggest fans remain those who are household names in pop themselves. Alvin Stardust used to stand in front of a mirror at home, armed with a tennis racket, imitating the Elvis Presley he'd seen only on films.

Les Gray, of Mud, is not only an Elvis addict, but he has deliberately put on an Elvis voice on records which have taken Mud right to the top of the charts. 'A tribute of my very own', he says.

When touring the States, Ian Hunter of Mott the Hoople was determined enough in his admiration of Elvis to reach Graceland's back door – only to be politely turned away by the maid.

The astonishing thing about Elvis's big-name fan club – and it even extends into the movie world, where Marlon Brando, for example, is an avowed Presley fanatic – is that so many of the 'members' are that much more versatile than Presley himself.

There may be only a handful who can come anywhere near to his on-stage performances, and only a tiny few would even want to have been involved in so many movies over so few years, but in musical terms, many have more strings to their bow than Elvis.

That Elvis gets so high in popularity polls for his guitar playing can be put down to the sheer blind enthusiasm of the hard-core fans. Few in-pop people have praised his playing, even though he spent a lot of time studying as a young man. And he really doesn't get much involved in songwriting.

Singing is clearly his business and in that he is probably the most versatile of them all.

By using top backing musicians, and top engineers, and by accepting advice from others, he has been at the centre of pop development. It is the fact that he was the first, that he pioneered the whole thing, that has given him so many pop-star followers.

Many, in all honesty, just about gave up on Presley during those rather barren years of the 1960s, and admitted that he had pushed out just money-making pulp – both on record and on film. But it was what went before, when he had the whole pop scene in a grip of steel, that kept their loyalty.

It surely takes a very special kind of pop performer to do that.

THOUGH it seems ludicrous to suggest that Elvis Presley was ever limited as a pop superstar, the fact is that most singers are only as good as their songs. And as he didn't produce much in the way of his own songs, then his hits had rub-off prestige for many top writers.

Altogether Elvis had recorded more than 800 titles by the time he'd been in the business twenty years. Many an unknown songwriter was suddenly pitchforked into fame and fortune because they happened to play a demonstration disc to the Elvis entourage at precisely the right time.

A girl named Ruth Bachelor is just one, and there aren't that many girl writers among the list. She is a journalist, a singer who has made her own records, and she writes poetry, designs for high-fashion outlets – and very much a Women's Liberationist.

She got on well with Elvis, who actually wanted to date this dark-haired and vivacious girl. She played him her song 'King Of The Whole Wide World', which was in the *Kid Galahad* movie, and it became a single and a hit for her. It meant that the name Ruth Bachelor suddenly meant a great deal in the songwriting industry.

Since then Ruth Bachelor has had her songs sung by stars like Jack Jones, Cliff Richard and Andy Williams, but Elvis was the real springboard to fame for her. Her songs appeared in *Girls! Girls! Girls!* and *It Happened At The World's Fair* as well as *Kid Galahad*. She's just the same age as Elvis. She says, 'Now I've hit the 40 mark I find the creative urge gets stronger and stronger.'

A team of an Irishman (Phil Coulter) and a Scotsman (Bill Martin) had great songwriting success long before Elvis Presley took one of their songs. But the thrill of having him cover the number, 'My Boy', still remains with them.

In fact, 'My Boy' provided Elvis with his biggest single hit in five years, so it was quite an achievement. Martin and Coulter wrote 'Puppet On A String', which was to be a world-seller through success in the European-linked Eurovision Song Contest. By the time Elvis took their ditty, they'd sold perhaps 40 million records of their songs round the world.

But even to them, Elvis Presley was 'different'. Martin says:

When we heard he'd been doing the song in his stage act, we flew straight to Las Vegas to try to see him and get him to release it as a single.

However as the whole world knows it is not easy to get to see Elvis, no matter who you may think you are. So we had to return to London. We figured we'd lost the battle but could go on to win the war.

In the end, they did win – by writing at least once a week to Colonel Parker, suggesting that the song should be released. Their letters remained unanswered but the song was put out on a single and it fairly zoomed up the charts. They never got a letter thanking them but the royalty cheques that started coming in from all over the world in 1974 were thanks enough. Bill adds, 'When I started out, I was desperate to be a songwriter. Just to have my name on a record was enough; I didn't care whether the song made me one pound or a million. Being on an Elvis hit was just great.'

The remarkably successful team of Jerry Leiber and Mike Stoller met up as two seventeen-year-old blues fans, and they decided to write songs. From 1954, they were immersed in the business. Their records with the Coasters remain all-time classics – songs like 'Charlie Brown', 'Along Came Jones', 'Yakety Yak', 'Poison Ivy' and 'Little Egypt'.

SONGWRITERS

Later they were to work with Elvis Presley at RCA Victor. They wrote and produced some of his big ones, like 'Santa Claus Is Back In Town', and the much-praised 'Jailhouse Rock'. And today they don't deny that being involved with Elvis is no handicap to finding fame and fortune.

For Elvis they turned out 'King Creole', 'Hound Dog', 'Hot Dog', 'Loving You', 'I Want To Be Free'.

By way of return, Elvis's hits produced a fortune for two guys who can still walk down any street anywhere and not be recognized. Says Leiber, 'We'd hate to be recognized all the time. That brings its own problems as Elvis knows all too well. But there can be no dispute that when he recorded "Hound Dog", it put us on the way upwards.'

Lieber and Stoller were in a sense soulmates of Elvis. They had been born white men, but loved the excitement and essential differences of the black man's musical world.

Strangely enough, Elvis has often publicly envied them. He says, 'It has to be a great feeling for a guy to be able to write songs that will be performed by a whole host of big names.'

There are big names and unknowns among the Elvis song list. Some do bear his own name. 'Aloha-Oe', for instance, was a traditional Hawaiian song which Elvis adapted to suit himself. He also arranged 'By and By', and gets his name as co-writer of 'Don't Be Cruel', along with Otis Blackwell. Elvis also arranged 'I'll Take You Home Again Kathleen', an old Irish number.

'Swing Low Sweet Chariot', an old Gospel number, is also credited to Elvis as arranger and adapter. As is 'O Come All Ye Faithful', one of his adaptations of a traditional hymn. And he co-wrote the pleasing 'That's Someone You Never Forget'.

Otherwise he had drawn his material from all sources. From long-established writers of 'standards' such as Cole Porter and Rodgers and Hammerstein and, in the rock field, Chuck Berry, another significant early influence.

In short, many songwriters have reason to be extra grateful to Elvis Presley. Being Elvis Presley can help a lot of people, simply by the association of his name.

But if Elvis at 20 was just starting out, at 30 was a legend and at 40 was setting new standards in terms of money-making success, then what about the Presley of 1985, when he will be 50 years old?

There will, certainly, be no need for him to still be working by then. But if he was still singing, then it could well be in the Gospel field. Perhaps not even for hard cash; just for the sake of putting something back into the church which inspired him early on.

In 1967, Elvis Presley brought out his *How Great Thou Art* album. The titles were: 'How Great Thou Art'; 'In The Garden'; 'Somebody Bigger Than You And I'; 'Farther Along'; 'Stand By Me'; 'Without Him'; 'So High'; 'Where Could I Go But To The Lord'; 'By And By'; 'If The Lord Wasn't Standing By My Side'; 'Run On'; 'Where No One Stands Alone'; and 'Crying In The Chapel'.

It was by no means one of his biggest-selling albums, but Elvis has often said that it was one of the most satisfying to record. And in early days, he really wanted to get into the Gospel field. In fact he once went for an audition for a Gospel group in Memphis – and, amazingly, was turned down. Perhaps it was just the way he looked, with the long hair, the sideburns and the garish clothes.

Now Gospel music is a popular area of popular music. J. D. Sumner has worked with Elvis on tour and in Vegas, along with his own group, the Stamps Quartet. He says:

Nobody could tell what might have happened had Elvis stuck more to the Gospel music. Maybe there would have been the same kind of boom in that kind of sound in the mid-fifties as there was in rock and roll. In fact our music, Gospel music, can be just as jivey as rock and roll.

There's black Gospel and white Gospel. We don't really try to save the people we sing to. Like Elvis, we are principally there to entertain. I wish everyone WAS saved, but my thing is not a church ministry.

Elvis could quite easily have stuck with Gospel music. He had, and has, the flair for it. In Britain, top pop singer Cliff Richard has gone more and more into religious areas, giving up much of his time for the church, and accompanying Billy Graham on his crusades. He has said, 'This way I give back something to the church which has been my inspiration.'

Elvis has undeniably been very religious from an early age. His mother was religious, too. When

TO THE KING

the early criticism of his appearance and his gestures came from churchmen, he was deeply hurt. He said he would not do anything to offend his own religious principles.

So it could just be that Elvis Presley, once the urge to perform in rock and roll has finally passed, could become a kind of evangelical soothsayer, because for sure he could 'spread the word' to more people than most in that field.

But this is mere guesswork. He could leave show business altogether. At 50, he could be just too tired to carry on doing anything.

What is certain is that when Elvis Presley does 'hang up his tonsils', as he once threatened to in 1968, he will still be talked about as the greatest single phenomenon in pop-music history.

T HE problem with finalizing statistics in the pop-music world is that they change so fast. One new single can add at least a million sales to an artist's tally. A break-off point has to be found. With Elvis Presley, his 40th birthday is at least a neatly marked career point.

By then, Elvis Presley had certainly sold in excess of 250 million worldwide. That averages out at well over ten million a year.

Certainly he had the greatest number of million-selling records in the USA for an individual by 1973 – no less than 27. The Beatles had more, with 37, but were to fade at the time Elvis was gaining new strength.

GOLD

In the States, the only audited measure of million-selling records is by the Recording Industry Association of America, and their awards did not start until 1958. Before that the awards were made on an informal basis – which means that unofficially Elvis Presley would have overtaken the Beatles, who did not start making hits until 1963.

By 1960, Bing Crosby had been awarded a platinum disc for sales of 200 million records sold.

So, although it is difficult to work out exact figures, in terms of 'gold' awards, length of time as a recording artist, and volume of sales at world level, Presley emerges as champion. His 'Hard-Headed

DISC

Woman', from the movie *King Creole*, was one of the first RIAA-certified gold awards made.

Though a comparison with the Beatles is difficult to make, since they were a group and Elvis is an individual, there is no doubt that their huge sales over a short period were very much due to the impact he had made seven years earlier in triggering off the whole rock and roll boom.

The Book Of Golden Discs, compiled by Joseph Murrells, gives the top five artists/groups in the million-selling list as at January 1971: 1. Elvis Presley (65, including five albums and one EP); 2. The Beatles, (59, including 20 albums and 3 EPS); 3. Fats Domino (23);

CHAMPION

4, Bing Crosby (22, including one album); 5, The Rolling Stones (21, including 7 albums).

Again, these figures are hard to bring completely up to date.

Bing Crosby's 'White Christmas', reissued virtually every December, has sold more than 30 million copies and his 'Silent Night' has almost reached that figure. But they reached 'gold' status back in 1942, when Presley was only a seven-year-old kid. His 'It's Now Or Never' sold more than 20 million worldwide in just a couple of years.

An analysis of records by various artists in the US Top Hundred as printed by *Billboard* from 1955 to 1972, with points awarded for positions reached, puts Elvis Presley at the top well in front of the Beatles – by 1,790 to 960. And during that period he had easily the greatest number of charted record sides, 130 – against runner-up James Brown, with 75.

He had the most Top Ten records (38, as compared to the Beatles' 31), though the Beatles pipped him in the number of Number One records, 20 as against 14.

Only Andy Williams equalled Presley, in the same breakdown, in number of years consecutively on the chart in America – both on 17, from 1956 to 1972.

In one spell of just fourteen months, Presley broke every possible attendance record in Las Vegas, pulled in 200,000 customers for six shows at the Houston Astrodome, had three million-selling singles, three albums which sold more than a million dollars' worth of copies – each!

In the UK between 1960 and 1973, Presley had 37 albums in the Top Twenty lists, though only five topped the chart. Top British artist over that period was Cliff Richard (17), who tied with the Rolling Stones.

Elvis's *Aloha From Hawaii* concert, relayed via satellite round the world, was seen by one-and-a-half BILLION people on the various showings. And the double album *Elvis: Aloha From Hawaii* was a qualified gold disc before the actual show was transmitted, just on advance orders from the shops.

Following Elvis Presley's first hit singles for RCA Victor, the company signed him to a 20-year contract – involving a great deal of money and an unprecedented act of faith in a comparatively unknown artist.

Presley is extremely generous and donates regularly to big American charities, gifts of $10,000 being commonplace.

Zooming out of Graceland to the waiting fans

He hit his 100 million disc sales in just eight years in the States, which worked out that one Elvis record was sold to somebody every two seconds – yet for two years of that time he was away in the Army.

One radio station in Honolulu once broadcast a non-stop session of Elvis records which went on for 78 hours.

Even when Japanese singer Kyu Sakamoto surprisingly hit the top spot in the American charts in 1963 with 'Sukiyaki', he insisted that Elvis Presley was his greatest influence.

On the commercial side, there have been times in recent years when there have been more than 80 different Presley products on the market, from dark-glow posters to lipsticks presented under such names as Hound Dog Orange.

The partnership of Presley and Parker has linked the other two 'P's' – product and promotion – and one of the most prophetic utterances in pop history must have been Parker's 1954 classic, 'You stay talented and sexy, and I'll make us both rich as rajahs'.

It is a partnership which has been based on tough dealing but complete honesty and trust. Though there have been many obvious mistakes, in terms of shoddy movies and not-so-hot records, the financial side has been organized with sheer genius. Perhaps that is the one weakness: Colonel Parker is financially inclined, not artistically attuned.

Just one thing is said to worry Elvis Presley, apart from the momentary and passing problems which his international status constantly throws up. He dreads the thought that he could end up with nothing because of getting into a muddle over his income tax. So he invites the Inland Revenue people to handle his returns and check his books. He says, 'I want to be sure I'm paying everything I owe. I think anybody who lives in a country should pay up the proper taxes. It's only fair that if you are earning the money, then you should pay your share to the Government.'

But the final summing up of Presley has to be that there can never be another artist to exert the same influences – even though others may achieve greater riches, faster.

Presley took an ailing, simpering, schmaltzy pop music industry by the scruff of the neck and changed everything for a whole generation. He's had more than his share of blame for matters often outside his control.

So it is only right that he should be acknowledged as . . . the King. Monarchs make mistakes, have lapses. But once it is there, the royal blood continues coursing through the veins.

At a Hollywood party with Frank and Nancy Sinatra and Fred Astaire